Responsive E-Government

ALSO BY NELS LINDAHL

Non-Fiction Books

Graduation with Civic Honors

Responsive E-Government

Fleeting Culture

Fiction Books

Forbidden Stones

Jupiter Darkly

United Earth Movement

Upper Bound Chronicles

Dream Chaser Archives

Call Center Days

Clandestine Offer

Responsive E-Government
A Study of Local Government E-Feedback Methodology

By Nels Lindahl

Responsive E-Government
A Study of Local Government E-Feedback Methodology

Published by Nels Lindahl

Printed in the United States of America

"It takes someone willing to work just beyond the edge of what is possible to accomplish something meaningful."

~ Nels Lindahl ~

Dedication

To Joni, Susan, Paul, Boyd, Jenifer, Gus Jr., Jason, Ben, Jim, Cheryl, Gus Sr., Joe, Bev, Twila, and John for providing support and information.

Dear reader,

Please enjoy this version of my dissertation.

Dr. Nels Lindahl, MPA, Ph.D.
Colorado Springs, Colorado
January 29, 2011

Abstract

Local governments have increased the use of technology (e-government) to gather citizen input. The current literature does not address the effectiveness, actual usage, or importance of electronic citizen feedback (e-feedback) to make policy decision. The purpose of the exploratory correlational study was to provide initial empirical evidence to assess the relationship between local e-government services and e-feedback collection methods. General theories of e-government practice were synthesized into a conceptual framework addressing research questions related usage of e-government, e-feedback and testing associations indicating that e-feedback was employed to guide e-government. A survey that documented current e-feedback collection methods and e-government services was sent to key informants representing a random sample of 174 principle cities of metropolitan and micropolitan statistical areas within the United States. Descriptive results indicated e-government was only 48% implemented across the sample with a potential expected expansion to 72%. Multiple linear regression analyses of survey items were used to identify significant predictors of current e-government and e-feedback practices; and parallel analyses were used to identify significant predictors of intended e-government and e-feedback practices. Pearson correlations were used to reveal significant linkages connecting e-government, e-feedback, and auditing e-feedback. The results support the conclusion that e-feedback methods create the potential for increased citizen influence in shaping government services and practices via the e-government model. The study contributes to positive social change by providing empirical data that can be used to guide initial e-government implementation within communities that have not yet adequately defined models of practice and means of gathering input from their citizenry.

Dedication
To my patient and understanding wife Joni, and anyone willing to
work just beyond the edge of what is possible.

Acknowledgments

I would like to acknowledge the people who worked toward the endorsement of this dissertation project:

The dissertation editors from the Walden University writing center, including Annie Pezalla, Tobias Ball, and Johannah Bomster, deserve special thanks for providing advice and assistance.

Thanks to Dr. David Milen for providing methodological guidance during the development of the research methods chapter. Dr. David Milen also provided guidance in expanding the depth and breadth of the literature review chapter.

Thanks to Dr. Stephen Morreale for providing the insightful suggestion to clarify the dissertation topic by developing an executive summary PowerPoint presentation. This alternative communication method advanced the dissertation process significantly.

Thanks to Dr. Kirk Elliott for providing comments, suggestions, and oversight during the University Research Review process.

Table of Contents

DEDICATION VII

ABSTRACT..I

DEDICATION II

ACKNOWLEDGMENTS..II

LIST OF FIGURES IV

CHAPTER 1: INTRODUCTION TO THE STUDY..5

OVERVIEW...5
STATEMENT OF THE PROBLEM...7
THE NATURE OF THE STUDY..7
RESEARCH QUESTIONS 7
RESEARCH HYPOTHESES RELATED TO THE RESEARCH QUESTIONS 8
PURPOSE OF THE STUDY 9
SIGNIFICANCE OF THE STUDY 9
   Professional Application...9
   Contribution to Social Change 10
BACKGROUND OF THE STUDY 10
   Traditional Feedback Methods 10
   Responsive E-Government Research 11
THEORETICAL BASE 12
   Stage 1: Data Collection...13
   Stage 2: Performance Evaluation 15
   Stage 3: Performance Improvement 15
DEFINITION OF TERMS...16
ASSUMPTIONS, LIMITATIONS, SCOPE, AND DELIMITATIONS.................................17
CHAPTER SUMMARY..18

CHAPTER 2: LITERATURE REVIEW 19

LITERATURE REVIEW STRUCTURE...19
   Literature Review Strategy..20
   Relevance to the Research Question..20
FEEDBACK METHODS 21
DEVELOPING TECHNOLOGY 24
E-GOVERNMENT..25
PERFORMANCE MEASUREMENT 27
TECHNOLOGICAL ACCEPTANCE MODEL...28
ORGANIZATIONAL SYSTEMS THEORY 29
ONLINE METHODS OF CITIZEN PARTICIPATION 30
   E-Commerce..31
   E-Research..31
   E-Voting 31
   E-Governance 32
   E-Democracy 32

Political Weblogs *33*
ETHICAL CONSIDERATIONS 34
Digital Divide...*35*
Access, Usability, and Trust...*36*
REVIEW OF METHODS..38
SUMMARY 39

CHAPTER 3: RESEARCH METHOD **41**

REVIEW OF RESEARCH METHODS OF RELATED STUDIES 41
RESEARCH QUESTIONS 41
Research Questions and Outcomes...*42*
Research Hypotheses Related to the Research Questions *42*
OPERATIONAL VARIABLE 43
Dependent Variables..*44*
Independent Variables *45*
Control Variables...*45*
RESEARCH DESIGN 45
SETTING AND SAMPLE 47
Sample Characteristics *47*
Study Population..*47*
Sampling Method *47*
Sample Size *48*
Participant Eligibility Criteria..*49*
SURVEY INSTRUMENT 49
Type of Survey Instrument..*49*
Survey Procedures *50*
Survey Reliability *50*
Survey Validity *51*
Survey Bias..*51*
Survey Completion *51*
Concepts Measured by the Survey *51*
Data Availability..*53*
Survey Testing Method..*54*
DATA COLLECTION..54
Survey Data From the Census of Government...*55*
Local Government Grouping Protocol *56*
STATISTICAL ANALYSIS...56
Data Analysis for Research Questions 1–3..*57*
Data Analysis for Research Question 4 ....*60*
Data Analysis for Research Question 5 ....*60*
FINDINGS PRESENTATION 61
ETHICAL PROTECTION OF PARTICIPANTS 61
CHAPTER SUMMARY..61

CHAPTER 4: RESULTS **63**

OVERVIEW OF THE CHAPTER 63
PROCEDURAL SURVEY NOTES 63

SURVEY RESPONSE RATE 64

ADHERING TO THE FINDINGS PRESENTATION 64

RESEARCH QUESTION 1 RESULTS 65

RESEARCH QUESTION 2 RESULTS 75

RESEARCH QUESTION 3 RESULTS 86

RESEARCH QUESTION 4 RESULTS 101

RESEARCH QUESTION 5 RESULTS 102

SURVEY DATA FROM THE CENSUS OF GOVERNMENT 103

LOCAL GOVERNMENT GROUPING PROTOCOL 104

CHAPTER SUMMARY 108

CHAPTER 5: CONCLUSIONS 109

STUDY OVERVIEW 109

RESEARCH METHODS 109

INTERPRETATION OF FINDINGS 110

Findings for Research Question 1 ....*110*

Findings for Research Question 2 ....*111*

Findings for Research Question 3 ....*112*

Findings for Research Question 4 ....*113*

Findings for Research Question 5 ....*113*

IMPLICATIONS FOR SOCIAL CHANGE 113

Professional Application..*114*

Contribution to Social Change *114*

RECOMMENDATIONS FOR ACTION AND FURTHER STUDY 114

CONCLUDING STATEMENT 115

REFERENCES 117

ABOUT THE AUTHOR 126

List of Figures

Figure 1. Three-stage e-government feedback model......................13

Figure 2. Measured elements. 52

Figure 3. Histogram of e-government (now). 66

Figure 4. Histogram of e-government (future). 67

Figure 5. Histogram of e-feedback (now). 77

Figure 6. Histogram of e-feedback (future)...................................78

Figure 7. Histogram of auditing e-feedback (now). 88

Figure 8. Histogram of auditing e-feedback (future). 89

Figure 9. Local government data four-variable comparison scatter
plot...105

Figure 10. Histogram of total population......................................106

Figure 11. Histogram of total housing units. 107

Figure 12. Histogram of median household income.......................108

Chapter 1: Introduction to the Study
Overview

A responsive electronic government (e-government) featuring electronic feedback (e-feedback) methodology provides local government with the mechanisms necessary to engage actively in the process of informed decision making. E-feedback evaluates the preferences of participants, in this case, citizens. Gladwell (2005) discussed the complexity of initial reactions within the decision-making process. However, public management stands on a tradition of informed decision making (McNabb, 2002). This study catalogued current e-feedback collection methods within e-government implementations in local governments with the largest populations in the United States. E-government involves the provision of government services online, utilizing citizen access through the Internet (Ho, 2002; Moon, 2002; West, 2004).

Collecting citizen feedback about local government matters and merits serious academic inquiry. Specifically, responsive e-government and the collection of e-feedback matters within the context of local government (Aikins & Krane, 2005). Responsive e-government can help local governments improve the process of informed decision making, increasing communication through feedback cycles and increasing citizen outreach (Coursey & Norris, 2008; Dalehite, 2008; Fountain, 2001). The implementation of e-government within local governments matters, because it formalizes bureaucracy and establishes the rules that form the basis of automating government services.

The theoretical basis of the study was that a special-case e-government scenario exists with respect to collecting citizen feedback online. General theories about the implementation of e-government services exist within the public administration literature (McNabb, 2002). This study focused on a special-case scenario that occurs when citizen feedback occurs online (i.e., e-feedback) after the implementation of e-government services within local governments in the United States.

Increasing citizen satisfaction with current e-government implementations will require governmental entities to gather e-feedback from citizens in response to calls for accountability and responsiveness in local government. Determining current levels of citizen satisfaction with government services and policies is critical, not only to identify changes in citizen satisfaction but also to model the changes in citizen satisfaction over time (Aikins, 2008). E-government implementations will have to include e-feedback collection methods to optimize online service delivery.

Norris and Lloyd (2006) suggested future research should supplement a knowledge gap in the academic literature related to theory development and theory testing. In addition to theory, Coursey and Norris (2008) suggested future research within the field of e-government should focus on addressing a knowledge gap in the academic literature through empirical data collection. With respect to the concerns of Norris and Lloyd as well as Coursey and Norris, a study that catalogs e-feedback collection methods within current e-government implementations will provide the data necessary to look at current e-feedback collection practices. Decision-makers can construct performance-measurement policies that use numerical optimization models to maximize potential citizen satisfaction. Expressions of citizen preference or opinion illustrate the direction a participant elects (Babbie, 2002). Integrated e-government implementations with e-feedback mechanisms provide the possibility of collecting information about citizen preferences with respect to governmental services and performance, ultimately a tool for improvement of accountability at all levels of government.

I utilized a survey to study the collection of e-feedback within current e-government implementations. Completing this study required survey questions to establish what e-government services local governments are using. A set of questions collected information about what citizen feedback mechanisms local governments utilize. The study involved collecting local government administrator preferences about the implementation of both e-government services and feedback collection methods.

Questions about the nature of citizen participation exist throughout democratic societies. With respect to the broader questions involved within the research, this study is relevant to a diverse group. Specifically, the study is relevant to citizens and community organizers interested in defined methods of participation within local government. A defined methodology for participation creates a definitive scenario for citizens to participate and provide feedback (Aikins, 2008). Additionally, local government practitioners interested in implementing and studying best-practice models dealing with citizen-feedback collection within e-government implementations should be interested in the study. Academics interested in the study of preference-based or informed decision making can utilize the data collected during the course of the study.

Further, academics interested in the study of e-government can evaluate this special-case scenario related to e-feedback. Finally, politicians focused on increasing citizen participation and satisfaction could be interested in the study.

Statement of the Problem

General theories about the implementation of e-government services exist within the public administration literature; however, specifically regarding citizen feedback about local government implementations of e-government utilizing e-feedback, very few extant studies used empirical or quantitative methodologies. The research problem addressed in this study is that lack of research on local government implementations of e-government utilizing e-feedback. I focused on a special-case scenario that develops when the collection of citizen feedback occurs online after the implementation of e-government services within local governments. I employed a quantitative field survey for analysis of local e-government implementations that utilize e-feedback. Information from the survey can help researchers analyze how local governments use, and intend to use, e-feedback to improve the experiences of citizens and to assist public administrators and other officials in making informed decisions and enhancing public policy.

The Nature of the Study

The research design involved implementing a quantitative, descriptive field survey to collect information not available in current research studies. Statistical analysis included descriptive measures and correlation tests. To accomplish the data collection, a field survey involving a self-administered questionnaire documented the current state of e-feedback collection methods and e-government services. Question design included a matrix format and a 7-point semantic, differential scale. More detailed discussion of the research methods is included in Chapter 3.

Research Questions

This study addressed an overarching area of research involving the process of implementing e-feedback mechanisms and developing auditing functions using such e-feedback. To address the formation of a bureaucratic structure around e-feedback the study examined the extent to which the presence of e-feedback mechanisms within local e-government implementations indicates the development of bureaucracy based on such e-feedback. The study was guided by five research questions:

1. To what extent do local governments utilize e-government?

2. To what extent do local governments utilize e-feedback?

3. To what extent do local governments audit the information collected from e-feedback implementations?

4. Does a statistically significant, positive relationship exist between the implementation of local e-government services and e-feedback collection methods that increase governmental responsiveness through citizen participation?

5. Does a statistically significant, positive relationship exist between the implementation of local e-feedback mechanisms and auditing functions utilizing the information collected from e-feedback mechanisms?

Research Hypotheses Related to the Research Questions

Within the framework of conducting academic research, a proposition defines a testable true-or-false statement. Cooper and Schindler (2003) defined a hypothesis as a proposition formulated for empirical testing. The following hypotheses and null hypotheses are based on the research questions:

H1. The local government has implemented e-government services.

$H1_0$. The local government has no e-government services implemented.

H2. The local government has implemented e-feedback mechanisms.

$H2_0$. The local government has no e-feedback mechanisms implemented.

H3. The local government uses the information collected from e-feedback mechanisms to fulfill auditing functions.

$H3_0$. The local government does not use information collected from e-feedback mechanisms to fulfill auditing functions.

H4. A statistically positive relationship exists between the implementation of local e-government services and e-feedback collection methods that increase responsiveness through citizen participation.

$H4_0$. No statistically positive relationship exists between the implementation of local e-government services and e-feedback collection methods that increase responsiveness through citizen participation.

H5. A statistically positive relationship exists between the implementation of local e-feedback mechanisms and auditing functions utilizing the information collected from e-feedback mechanisms.

$H5_0$. No statistically positive relationship exists between the implementation of local e-feedback mechanisms and auditing functions utilizing the information collected from e-feedback mechanisms.

Purpose of the Study

This study helped identify factors that influence the implementation of e-feedback collection methods based on e-government. The development of empirical evidence will continue to advance contemporary research into e-government (Coursey & Norris, 2008). Understanding how local governments utilize e-feedback mechanisms will help advance future research into modeling changes in citizen satisfaction, contributing to responsive e-government performance improvement in the future. Additional research focusing on e-government should work toward theory development and theory testing, which will reduce gaps in the literature (Norris & Lloyd, 2006). Responsive e-government has the potential to strengthen the participatory nature of democracy by increasing citizen participation. Scholars and practitioners working within the field of public administration or public policy in general need mechanisms for utilizing citizen feedback. E-government implementations can collect e-feedback from citizens to increase citizen satisfaction.

Significance of the Study

Putnam (2000) argued that increasing citizen participation in government is a significant and meaningful challenge. Declines in citizen participation within democratic process risk the foundations of democracy (Barber, 1984; Macedo, 2005; Skocpol, 2003). This study contributes to the literature by expanding understanding of how current e-government implementations utilize e-feedback methods. Understanding how to improve online service delivery contributes to positive social change by facilitating citizen participation in government. Practitioners within the field of public administration need mechanisms for utilizing e-feedback to increase citizen satisfaction.

Professional Application

Practitioners will benefit from the advancement of theory development and theory testing. Norris and Lloyd (2006) suggested that academics within the field of public administration focusing on e-government should work toward theory development and theory testing. Practitioners also will benefit from empirical data collection. Increasing the available information about e-government will help administrators improve the decision-making process. Coursey and

Norris (2008) identified a knowledge gap related to empirical data collection about e-government.

Contribution to Social Change

Increased governmental responsiveness directly benefits citizens. Online services provide citizens direct access to government and serves to promote social change by improving the opportunity for constituency input (Fountain, 2001). E-government implementations with e-feedback collection methods allow citizen participation in government in a venue other than direct personal interaction. Putnam (2000) theorized that greater citizen participation in government strengthens the fabric of representative democracy.

Background of the Study

Researchers have noted the importance of civic engagement and citizen participation within civil society to strengthening democracy through civic renewal (Dionne, 1998; Putnam, 2000; Sirianni & Friedland, 2001; Skocpol, 2003). At the same time, political scandals have decreased public trust in government, resulting in a decline in voting, campaigning, and discourse (McLean, Schultz, & Steger, 2002). Town hall meetings traditionally have provided a forum for public meetings within the United States. Sennett (1992) argued that even the idea of public is ending as electronic communication increases. The possibility for individual political participation diminishes when town hall meetings or public meetings transition from local events to nationally televised political productions. At the same time, general access to information is increasing. Access to e-government implementations provides any individual with direct access to both government services and community officials. E-government represents a modern method of citizen access to government beyond the traditional constraints of town hall or public meetings.

Traditional Feedback Methods

Local U.S. governments are interacting with citizens using e-government implementations. All interactions between government and citizens present the possibility of collecting feedback (Aikins, 2008). A study of utilization of e-government services would be a study of citizen interaction with government (Ho & Ni, 2004). E-government has changed the nature of public meetings by providing a forum for the exchange of information without the constraints of traditional town-hall-style meetings (Hanson, 2003). Before the advent of e-government, different factors contributed to the breakdown of civic participation in the democratic process (Putnam,

2000). Sennett (1992) predicted that traditional, face-to-face, social networks would have a diminished value, due to increases in available information about social groups that reduce the need for face-to-face contact. Instant access to information has limited the need for traditional organizations to engage in practical face-to-face networking. As technology intersects with modernity, the Internet influences both democracy and public spaces (Chambers, 2005).

Responsive E-Government Research

Norris and Lloyd (2006) suggested future research should supplement a knowledge gap in the academic literature related to theory development and theory testing. In addition to theory, Coursey and Norris (2008) suggested future research within the field of e-government should focus on addressing a knowledge gap in the academic literature through empirical data collection. Based on the research of Coursey and Norris, the collection of empirical data about e-government represents a significant gap in the literature. Responsive e-government can strengthen the fabric of democracy by answering public questions of effectiveness, increasing citizen participation in the administrative process, and delivering empirical data to improve administrative decision making. This research helps fill a gap in current literature by determining what online methods local governments use to collect e-feedback to empower responsive e-government. Identifying the currently implemented combinations of e-feedback methods allows for the optimization of e-government and identifies opportunities for strengthening responsive e-government. Without responsive e-government, citizens may perceive online platforms as an impediment, if they appear to deny citizens a direct path to share preferences with local governments (Perritt, 1997).

Technology developments can be modular in nature. Governments develop specific, task-oriented, service-delivery solutions to fulfill a particular need as identified by constituency research and interaction. Each service-delivery technology may be modular in design. Scholars have defined and explored the various ways e-government implementations evolve (Baum & Di Maio, 2000; Hiller & Belanger, 2001; Layne & Lee, 2001; Ronaghan, 2001; Wescott, 2001). West (2004) suggested e-government implementations tend to develop incrementally, moving in stages that include publishing information, developing interactive components, completing financial transactions, and finally integrating service delivery. E-government implementations typically follow a reasonable pattern of incremental development.

Dalehite (2008) and Wichowsky and Moynihan (2008) identified a trend toward performance measurement using citizen satisfaction as a baseline. Performance measurement trends include online surveys, online polling, benchmarking, website statistics, focus groups, mail surveys, phone surveys, virtual focus groups, performance measurement, internal staff evaluation, and independent auditing. A more substantial review of appropriate literature is presented in Chapter 2.

Theoretical Base

A special-case e-government scenario involves e-feedback. Within the public administration literature, general theories exist about implementing e-government services at the local government level (Norris & Lloyd, 2006). Specifically, this study focused on a special-case scenario involving e-feedback that occurred after the implementation of e-government services within local governments.

Cooper and Schindler (2003) suggested that models represent phenomena through analogy. Developing a clear theoretical base requires defining feedback collection, performance evaluation, and process improvement within the context of e-government implementations. E-feedback collection is a necessary part of gathering the information required to model changes in citizen satisfaction over time (Wichowsky & Moynihan, 2008). E-government implementations create the possibility of collecting information about citizen preferences by using e-feedback collection methods.

Cooper and Schindler (2003) defined the three major functions of models for applied research or theory building as (a) description, (b) explication, and (c) simulation. Within applied research or theory building, a descriptive model serves to establish the framework for additional research. Explicative models extend or expand previously developed models. Simulation-based modeling provides the possibility of examining relationships through clarification. The theoretical base for this study involved developing a three-stage model for maximizing citizen satisfaction using numerical optimization: (a) e-feedback data collection, (b) performance evaluation, and (c) performance improvement. This theoretical base is shown in Figure 1.

Figure 1. Three-stage e-government feedback model.

Stage 1: Data Collection

McNabb (2002) described the process of collecting primary data as gathering information that was not previously available. Glynn, Herbst, O'Keefe, and Shapiro (1999) evaluated the tradition of researchers evaluating public opinion. Information technology provides local government with the ability to use e-government implementations to collect primary data about citizen satisfaction. Coursey and Norris (2008) and Norris and Lloyd (2006) revealed that a wide variety of data collection methods is available, including traditional phone surveys, face-to-face interviews, and various online feedback methods.

Online feedback methods. Preference-based indictors provide measurable factors to describe decision making. A narrative thread running throughout this discussion details the potential influence of citizen preferences on administrative decision making. Interactive online systems provide the basis for developing dynamic, preference-based evaluation systems (Streib & Navarro, 2006). E-feedback mechanisms are an integral component for effective data collection in online environments (Aikins, 2008). Prior to access, the design and development of online feedback mechanisms may include the use of freeware, privately developed software, or open source software, depending in part on budget and technology staffing expertise (Lindahl, 2010). E-government provides a potentially powerful platform for data collection via online surveys, online polling, benchmarking, website statistics, focus groups, and virtual focus groups (West, 2004). Each of these e-feedback methods has the potential to collect data critical to the measurement of citizen satisfaction.

Local government, as an option, could deploy online surveys to collect information about citizen preferences. One advantage of online surveys is that surveys may allow for research without direct observation of the participants (Cooper & Schindler, 2003). Thus, the use of online surveys represents a method of research that requires depth without direct observation of the participating subject. Without face-to-face interaction, options for acquiring information include methods such as online polling to provide e-feedback from citizens about preferences regarding a specific issue or question (Thomas & Streib, 2005).

Ammons (2002) explained the process of utilizing performance-measurement techniques transitions into benchmarking applications based on comparing improvements. Website statistics provide a wealth of potential information about citizen preferences based on utilization (Wong & Welch, 2004). To provide further support for this method of data collection, Babbie (2004) explained that a research focus group involves bringing a relatively small group of people together to engage in facilitated discussion on specific topics. Virtual focus groups utilize the same framework for facilitating discussion using advanced technology. Independently auditing e-feedback collection methods requires special consideration.

Measuring citizen satisfaction. Performance measures can account for magnitude, effectiveness, and efficiency. Hernon (1994) provided a list of considerations for performance measures including appropriateness, validity, replication, comparability, and practicality. One of the outcomes associated with successful e-government implementation is citizen satisfaction. E-feedback collection methods provide a way to measure changes in citizen satisfaction. Dalehite (2008) suggested future research into citizen satisfaction should evaluate the influence of improvements in information quality.

Stage 2: Performance Evaluation

Performance measures allow the possibility of evaluation. Performance measurement provides accountability with the possibility of monitoring and improving services (Ammons, 2002). Hernon (1994) discussed how performance measures provide the evaluation tools necessary to improve accountability. Performance evaluation involves determining what factors contribute to changes in citizen satisfaction over time. The measured feedback provided becomes the basis of a performance-evaluation tool.

Dalehite (2008) presented evidence that performance measurement is moving beyond theoretical research and translating into a practical method for teaching, promotion, and implementation. Performance modeling involves comparing at least two potential solutions to determine which solution maximizes potential citizen satisfaction. The performance-modeling approach supports longitudinal research into maximizing potential citizen satisfaction.

Stage 3: Performance Improvement

Hernon (1994) argued that increased focus on satisfaction, quality, and performance improves the possibility of collecting reliable and valid data, allowing researchers to expand beyond descriptive statistics. Kelly and Swindell (2002) attempted to model the concept of citizen satisfaction. Management practices utilize various survey methodologies to improve performance. Currently, the budgetary process utilizes citizen surveys (Hassett & Watson, 2003). After building the theoretical case for the optimization of performance measurement, the theoretical base will have to move from theory to the practice of attempting to quantify specific variables at different points in time. By leveraging the combination of theory and practice, the theoretical base not only expands to include using e-feedback from citizens about e-government but also provides the information necessary to audit performance over time. Research from Ammons (2002) suggested systems of regular performance feedback to all levels of local government are possible. Additionally, Dalehite (2008) concluded that if information generated by performance systems does not produce usable results for decision making, then the potential for waste instead of efficiency exists. The summary of these observations served to inform the current research questions to fill a gap in current literature.

Definition of Terms

Benchmarking: Previously defined goals, objectives, and standards are used to measure organizational performance (Ronaghan, 2001).

Citizen satisfaction: The utility citizens derive from the functions of government (Welch, Hinnant, & Moon, 2005).

Digital divide: The separation between the total population of people with accessible Internet access and the population without Internet access (Belanger & Carter, 2009).

E-commerce: Electronic commerce; opportunity for fiscal transactions electronically through the Internet (Thomas & Streib, 2005).

E-democracy: Use of technology to engage in democratic practices (Thomas & Streib, 2005).

E-feedback: Electronic feedback; the implementation of feedback collection methods online to measure citizen presences about a specific topic (Lindahl, 2010).

E-governance: Provision of government electronically through the Internet (West, 2004).

E-government: Electronic government; the provision of government services electronically through the Internet (West, 2004).

E-research: Electronic research; ability to access information online for the purposes of conducting research (Thomas & Streib, 2005).

E-voting: Electronic voting; process of expressing preferences in a defined, measurable way (Moynihan, 2004).

Feedback loops: Process of collecting information for the purpose of evaluating and adjusting an ongoing operation (Barlow & Moller, 1996).

Independent auditing: Process of organizational evaluation by an independent, outside source (McNabb, 2002).

Internal staff evaluation: Process of organizational internal evaluation (Babbie, 2004).

Numerical optimization: Improvement through numerical comparison of various actions and alternatives (Bertilsson & Nilsson, 2004).

Online polling: Collecting selection-based preferences through online questions (Babbie, 2004).

Online surveys: Collecting preference-based opinion through online questions (McNabb, 2002).

Performance measurement: Evaluating performance based on measurable variables (Dalehite, 2008).

Virtual focus groups: Hosting traditional, preference-based focus groups through online forums (Putnam, 2000).

Website statistics: Descriptive report of various performance factors involved in the daily administration of a website (Wong & Welch, 2004).

Assumptions, Limitations, Scope, and Delimitations

The study was limited to analysis of current e-feedback methods that measure citizen satisfaction with local e-government implementations. The study was based on the assumption that metropolitan and micropolitan statistical areas in the United States represent cities with large populations, information-technology budgets, and e-government implementations. One of the problems facing the study was the assumption that the titles of certain feedback methods might not conform to a universal definition.

Potential weaknesses of the study include participant accuracy, language questions such as the prevalence of common definitions, and the potential benefits available from longitudinal variables within the study. Researchers assume all of the preferences expressed by a participant are accurate. Researchers have no method of verifying participant preferences. Size of the sample, verification of participants, and individual definition differences were limitations of the study. The survey methodology could have had different levels of participants within different organizations that might not be comparable. Finally, the study was limited to the e-government feedback collection methods of online surveys, online polling, benchmarking, website statistics, focus groups, mail surveys, phone surveys, virtual focus groups, performance measurement, internal staff evaluation, and independent auditing.

Each of the previously enumerated study weaknesses received attention and evaluation during the course of the study. Addressing participant accuracy involved using a survey pretest and limiting the scope of potential answers. Clear explanation and context helped overcome issues related to the prevalence of common definitions. Introducing the potential for study replication helped provide a potential response to questions about any preferences expressed by participants. Only the potential for future replication creates a scenario for testing the results and examining the methods utilized within the study.

Chapter Summary

Advancing e-government research will require cataloging e-feedback collection methods by local e-government implementations. Findings may serve to inform decision makers on ways to improve citizen satisfaction with current e-government implementations. In this study, cataloging e-feedback collection methods within e-government implementations provided the data necessary to look at current e-feedback collection practices. E-feedback allows decision makers to construct performance-measurement policies that use numerical optimization models to maximize potential citizen satisfaction.

Chapter 2 of the study provides a literature review of available public administration research. Chapter 3 provides details about the research methodology of the study. Chapter 4 provides results, and Chapter 5 concludes the study with recommendations for research and practice.

Chapter 2: Literature Review

Central to the foundation of the study, I conducted an exhaustive literature review of relevant e-feedback collection methods and e-government literature within the field of public administration. The literature included descriptions of various tools for managers to make decisions (Ammons, 2002). All of the current e-government implementations reviewed are illustrative of the results of completed decision-making processes. The structure and formality of e-government provide the possibility of public management reform through process transparency and definition (Asgarkhani, 2005). From a purely structural perspective, understanding how the current public administration literature addresses feedback collection methods and e-government can answer questions about the future path of e-government. Within the field of public administration, overspecialization will result in a complex fragmentation that precludes the adoption of integrated e-government services. Within the context of overspecialization, the researcher also needs to consider legal perspectives (Galindo, 2004). Given the aforementioned considerations, I evaluated the research in terms of online citizen participation methods within the context of e-government implementation.

Literature Review Structure

An analysis of the basic structure of the literature review, or a structural roadmap, provides the reader with a basic understanding of what has been included in the literature review. Researchers can study innovative theories to see what will happen next in terms of industry change (Christensen, Anthony & Roth, 2004). After the introductory section, the literature review begins with a discussion of the historical basis of feedback methods. Following this section is a section providing an overview discussion of technology within public administration literature. This section provides the context for the rest of the literature review. Given the rapid rate of change within discussions of technology, only overviews discussing the current state of the literature can provide the foundation necessary to delve into a higher degree of subject-matter specificity. The next section of the literature review evaluates the relevant e-government literature.

Several additional literature review topics deserve consideration, including performance measurement, the technological acceptance model, and organizational systems theory. Adding a degree of depth to the online methods of citizen participation previously enumerated in the literature, each of these areas of academic inquiry builds the foundation necessary to evaluate such methods. Beyond the introductory sections and subject overviews, the literature review begins a comprehensive analysis of the various online methods of citizen participation associated with e-government within the public administration literature. This area of the literature review contains the most depth and defines the very nature of how e-feedback mechanisms develop within current online citizen participation. Within this context, discussion of the online methods of citizen participation occurs with respect to the relevant public administration literature. Each online participation method represents a type of online implementation that allows citizens to interact with or utilize government. The final sections of the literature review cover ethical considerations and provide a review of the literature associated with the research methods employed in the study.

Literature Review Strategy

The basic structure of the literature review involves looking at specific technology, specific participation methods, and finally ethical considerations. The literature search involved relevant academic journals available through online databases including Political Science Complete, Sage Political Science Collection, Expanded Academic ASAP, SocINDEX, and the Military and Government Collection. Initially the search framework involved combinations of keywords related to both feedback collection methods and e-government within the public administration literature. Local government-based online methods of citizen participation are relevant to the study. The specific implementation methods under consideration included specific key terms: e-government, e-commerce, e-research, e-voting, e-governance, e-democracy, and political weblogs. Only certain segments of government accept each new technology. Any discussion of e-government has to address the digital divide, website usability, and relevant ethical issues associated with government development of technology.

Relevance to the Research Question

The public administration literature addressed the concept of e-government in detail. However, the scholarly literature within the field of public administration fell short of defining e-feedback collection mechanisms for interacting with citizens or measuring citizen satisfaction within e-government implementations. Only e-feedback mechanisms can provide researchers with the information

necessary to analyze e-government implementations (Aikins, 2008).
Definition and specificity within the development of online
government implementations can provide a mechanism for public
management reform (Asgarkhani, 2005).

Feedback Methods

Historically, local governments have been able to use a
variety of feedback collection methods, including modern e-feedback
mechanisms. Glynn et al. (1999) debated the nature and various
traditions of researchers' evaluations of public opinion. A multitude
of feedback collection methods exist within the United States,
including pamphleteering, personal letters, conventions, town
meetings, newspapers, public political debates, radio broadcasts,
televised town hall meetings, and national town hall meetings.

During the formation of the United States democratic
processes developed. Hundreds of years later, scholars (e.g., Barber,
1984; Macedo, 2005; Skocpol, 2003) now argue that declining
citizen participation in democratic processes puts the very foundation
of representative democracy at risk. Citizen participation in
government was necessary during the formational period. Inherent
within the initial functionality of government, citizen participation
brought together various democratic processes (Putnam, 2000).
Research available on the topic suggested that scholars believe even
the possibility of citizen participation in government deserves
consideration (Putnam, 2000; Skocpol, 2003).

At the most basic level of consideration or study, citizen
participation in government describes the first step in the process.
Essential to democracy and the basis of civil society is citizen
participation in the community, business, and government (Dionne,
1998). Scholars generally adopted a perspective that values citizen
participation (Van Til, 2000). Citizen participation is an important
part of the democratic process (Skocpol, 2003). Understanding
citizen participation requires understanding the history of how
participation developed, why people wanted to participate, and what
sustains interest in participation. If citizen participation is an
important part of the democratic process, then the historical
influences surrounding participation require definition and
consideration.

Considering the concept of civil society requires scholars to
be careful in upholding a consistent presentation and definition. Van
Til (2000) argued that theorists have to avoid using the concept of
civil society as a type of social-science clay that can be molded into

21

almost any shape. Reducing potentially problematic bias will involve keeping this conceptual issue in mind while addressing the issue of civil society and citizen participation (Putnam, 2000). Introducing concepts and ideas without providing detailed explanations or basic definitions creates a scenario where a lack of clear intent potentially clouds perception.

Part of the challenge of understanding town hall meetings involves identifying the relationship between technology and changes in citizen participation in government. Putnam (2000) observed that living alone and working late combined with television and the Internet have rendered society less trusting and less civic. The current trajectory of citizen participation in the democratic process is calling into question the future of democratic governance in the United States.

An historical perspective on citizen participation illustrates how town hall meetings are part of the democratic process. Finding ways to communicate ideas to the people required the use of technology like the printing press (Eisenstein, 1979). Frederickson (1997) argued that politics is a noble expression of collective cooperation. Consider the politics of major political figures who actively engaged in writing personal letters, public letters, and letters to newspapers. Skocpol (2003) used examples from history to illustrate the powerful possibilities of community action. From a historical perspective, one might examine the social connections that have driven not only the formation of the first elements of community activity but also legislative change. Examples exist throughout history, including town hall meetings led by Martin Luther King during the civil rights movement and the potential influence of modern citizens' groups (Putnam, 2000).

Frederickson (1997) observed that early politicians like Benjamin Franklin worked in the media publishing newspapers, magazines, pamphlets, and books. Newspapers provide the possibility of disseminating information to the community. Within the community, the shared perspective on an issue of importance describes the state of the public mind through defining a shared frame of reference. With respect to a shared frame of reference, Sennett (1992) noted that during the mid 18th century an audience could repeat certain phrases from debates and theater.

Frederickson (1997) argued that citizens previously functioned by taking direct collective action in the form of town meetings, militias, and community activities like a barn-raising.

Frederickson went as far as to draw the conclusion that the tradition of citizens choosing to engage in direct collective action has been lost. Representative democracy requires a mechanism for citizens to share ideas within a community. Town hall meetings are a way to facilitate citizen participation in the democratic process.

Large nations like the United States require the maintenance and availability of numerous methods of communication for participatory democracy to function. A society can neither forget the past nor ignore the future. Dionne (1998) argued that society has to recognize individuals and organizations that work toward building civil society. Public meetings, town meetings, or town hall meetings all represent a method of public assembly for the purpose of discourse within the community. Before the formalization of democratic institutions in the United States, the primary methods of political discourse involved informal communication. Communication is a necessary element of community.

At the heart of critical dialogue or discussion focused on methods of citizen feedback like town hall meetings is the observation about the lack of serious consideration for a nationwide system of local participation (Barber, 1984). Without a perceived need for a nationwide system of local participation, public demand does not spark action. Traditionally, citizen feedback occurs through town hall meetings or city council meetings (Barber, 1984). Outside public meetings, the major method local government uses to collect feedback is the citizen survey (Barber, 1984). A citizen survey can involve using focus groups, postal delivery paper surveys, or automated telephone surveys.

Information technology currently provides local government with the ability to use e-government implementations to collect primary data about citizen satisfaction. Coursey and Norris (2008) and Norris and Lloyd (2006) revealed that a wide variety of data collection methods is available, including traditional phone surveys, face-to-face interviews, and various online feedback methods. Modern feedback methods include Internet communication technology, Internet streaming audio and video, and online press conferences. E-government also provides a potentially powerful platform for data collection via e-feedback through online surveys, online polling, benchmarking, website statistics, and virtual focus groups.

Developing Technology

Scholarly research into technology within the field of public administration represents a relatively recent phenomenon. Adoption of technology within government depends on the degree of perceived usefulness (F. D. Davis, 1989). The initial adoption of various personal computer systems occurred during the 1990s (Brudney & Selden, 1995). E-government or the provision of government services online defines a large area of research developing between 1994 and 1999 (Ho, 2002). A difference exists between specific e-government service implementation and the processes of governing online, termed e-governance. Information technology has fundamentally changed governmental functions (Fountain, 2001). Government adoption of technology demonstrates a cause-and-effect relationship with organizational change and institutional change (Bretschneider, 2003; Fountain, 2001). In public administration, the advent of e-government is focusing already scarce resources on the incremental implementing new technology-based services and raising the level of sophistication of current services at all levels of government (Moon, 2002; Moynihan, 2004; Norris & Moon, 2005; West, 2004).

A combination of public expectations and potential benefits is driving public administration toward a path of technological acceptance in the name of innovation and progress (Fountain, 2001; Moynihan, 2004; Thomas & Streib, 2003). Integrating efficiency, economy, and social equity is one of the central challenges facing public administration (Frederickson, 1997). A history of the technological change associated with the e-government revolution highlights a series of management problems associated with realizing the potential for good government, increased transparency, greater access to information, and the potential for online civic participation. Within the emergency management literature, Waugh and Streib (2006) reported the benefits of leadership strategies toward developing a collaborative problem-solving mechanism. E-government literature is slowly moving from developmental considerations to informed decision making with collaborative possibilities. Van Wart (2003) provided a scathing account of public leadership theory within the public administration literature. According to Trottier, Van Wart, and Wang (2008), leadership remains a significant factor in the proper execution of public management strategies. E-government implementations are an example of where public leadership and administrative stewardship are necessary.

E-government discussions could start with an explanation of the basic economic principles of supply and demand. Citizens started to demand access to information and services online, and government responded by meeting that demand (Dalehite, 2008). Fountain (2001) suggested e-government could change democratic governance forever or simply could be a historical footnote in a very long timeline of specific government reforms. Future benefits must avoid potential conflicts with the value choices made during the e-government implementation and development process.

E-government has the potential to increase access to information and elected officials (Koh, Ryan, & Prybutok, 2005). Scholars in the field of public administration tend to analyze e-government by identifying different stages of e-government development as the primary unit of analysis (Norris & Lloyd, 2006). Determining what potential transformational effects e-government could have on democratic governance deserves extensive consideration and analysis (Fountain, 2001). A central question about e-government involves the difference between operating to satisfy citizen expectations and operating to provide services before citizen expectations develop.

Questions about technological efficiency require a synthesis of the history of how technological efficiency influences the machinery of government, specifically within the context of emerging e-government trends with respect to the interaction between ethics and technology. Online collaboration can occur though strategic alliances between nonprofits and business (Austin, 2000). Questions about why organizations decide to adopt specific technologies are appropriate during any stage of implementation or maintenance. Dugan (2002) considered the various challenges organizations face integrating technology-related costs into the budget. Serious budget considerations include the measurement of actual cost, return on investment, and accountability concerns. Public managers have to be decisive and control information technology (Barrett & Greene, 2001).

E-Government

Researchers studying e-government can focus on highly specific government functions limiting the scope of each article or study. Fragmented leadership on the issues has allowed knowledge-area specialization in the current e-government literature, creating extensive fragmentation (Norris & Lloyd, 2006). Perhaps this fragmentation is a result of a technology development timeline or a result of highly specialized funding and projects (Norris & Moon, 2005). At some point in the development of e-government literature, the various concepts that define online implementations will require integration into one best practice model replicated throughout state and local government.

Citizens favor the adoption and expansion of e-government implementations but are concerned about privacy (Blair, 2003). C. N. Davis (2005) suggested that privacy and access within e-government implementations could be reconciled. Defining the rules for e-government implementations provides the foundation for institutional change (Bretschneider, 2003). Before consideration of the potential for institutional change, Norris and Moon (2005) raised concerns about development strategies following the initial wave of e-government services as a part of efforts to increase e-government sophistication. Comparisons of e-government implementations require benchmarks that determine value and validity (Bannister, 2007).

West (2004) contended that online interactive features of e-government could promote responsiveness and public outreach while transforming service delivery. West adopted the perspective that new technology is allowing the development of e-government by transforming service delivery and changing citizen attitudes. Using the transformational influence of technology as a frame of reference, West looked at technological change in e-government while considering online privacy and security from a public perspective, focusing on addressing public concerns.

E-government implementations can be record-keeping and record-making systems (Barry, 2004). Inherent within this viewpoint are questions about personal privacy and security, requiring specific problem definitions and solutions that do not receive coverage within Barry's article. Scholars should use care to avoid focusing on the potential outcomes of e-government instead of the potential pitfalls that could occur during the process of e-government implementation. This scenario is analogous to an argument requiring justification to reach a conclusion: Research has to provide justification for any potential conclusion (McNabb, 2002). Ho and Ni (2004) evaluated the adoption of factors for various e-government features within Iowa county treasurers' offices. Based on definitive research, best practice models need to address issues such as reliability and

26

security, whereas personal privacy should be part of the design and implementation phases of e-government.

E-government implementations have the capacity to collect e-feedback from citizens. Each element of e-feedback from citizens provides a gift for public managers using feedback to improve both processes and decision making (Barlow & Moller, 1996). Public managers can design benchmarking systems and other methods of collecting the data necessary to demonstrate the effectiveness of e-government implementations (Beck, 2003).

Coursey and Norris (2008) suggested models for explaining e-government implementation require empirical study. At the same time, e-government models need to be reconciled with the possibility of increased accountability (Wong & Welch, 2004). Beck (2003) reported that e-government managers use benchmarks to define a project's success. Regardless of the potential modeling and best practices, Yu-Che and Thurmaier (2008) suggested the adoption of e-goverment implementions depends on budget considerations. Ya Ni and Bretschneider (2007) focused on the idea of contracting out e-government services. Budget considerations would affect signing multiple-year contracts for e-government services.

Performance Measurement

The wide variety of feedback collection methods include online surveys, online polling, benchmarking, website statistics, focus groups, mail surveys, phone surveys, virtual focus groups, internal staff evaluation, and independent auditing. Any of the feedback collection methods provides a possible mechanism for performance measurement. Decision makers have a wide variety of tools for decision making that require gathering information (Ammons, 2002). Dalehite (2008) suggested performance measurement techniques like citizen surveys should be an active part of the decision-making process.

Understanding the history of e-government involves looking at both changes in government and changes in technology. E-government mechanisms can facilitate public management reform (Asgarkhani, 2005). Public managers working with e-government have to document methods of proving a project's success (Beck, 2003). Managers at all levels of government face challenges in providing accountability and performance measures for developing technology. Websites can create digital records and display previously stored records digitally (Barry, 2004).

E-government benchmarking has the potential to create pressure on public managers (Bannister, 2007). Organizational goals and objectives change in connection with citizens' expectations for services online. The resulting need emerges for administrators who can adapt managerial techniques to developing technology to ensure good government. Finding ways to build performance measurements for developing technology can be difficult, because organizational leaders have to anticipate expectations and develop standards to meet those expectations. Wichowsky and Moynihan (2008) maintained that from a policy feedback perspective, potential performance management techniques influence political participation, social capital, and citizen satisfaction, underscoring the need for measurements, analysis, and adaptation.

Data collected from online performance measurement techniques enable numerical optimization of alternatives. Automatic optimization is possible through iterative trials using both software models and hardware computational efficiency measures (Bertilsson & Nilsson, 2004). Further, contracting out e-government services can reduce the ability of government to build accountability mechanisms into the process (Ya Ni & Bretschneider, 2007). E-government development has raised accountability and transparency concerns. Without strong accountability and transparency measures, e-government technology can simply sustain existing practices (Wong & Welch, 2004).

Technological Acceptance Model

Adoption and diffusion of information technology are the foundation of the technological acceptance model. Current models for administrative processes, including the technological acceptance model, developed from Lindblom's (1959) initial definition of the science of muddling through decision-making processes. The adoption of e-government initiatives creates finance challenges for local governments (Yu-Che & Thurmaier, 2008). Instead of looking at the incremental progression of developing technology, Fountain (2001) discussed the nature of enacted technology. Several scholars predicted that Internet technology would not transform democracy (R. Davis, 1999; Margolis & Resnick, 2000). However, all technology, including e-government, gradually and continuously evolves (Moon, 2002). Different size governments adopt information technology in different ways (Brudney & Selden, 1995). Norris and Kraemer (1996) determined that local governments with a central information technology department were more likely to adopt leading-edge technologies. Various views exist about how to evaluate perceptions of red tape and information technology innovations in organizations (Moon & Bretschneider, 2002). Moon and Norris (2005) studied the implementation of e-government, determining that a manager's level of innovation and city size are determinants of technological development.

Organizational Systems Theory

High-risk systems, high reliability, and error-free organization are frequently mentioned in the e-government literature. Moynihan (2004) focused the debate about security by comparing the differences between e-government and e-voting. Moynihan highlighted the need to understand the limitations and potential risks of adopting new technology from a systems theory perspective. By looking at the acceptance of technological innovation in service delivery, Moynihan was able to look beyond the public opinion concerns about personal privacy and securities expressed by West (2004) and to analyze the actual process using systems theory. Challenging the acceptance of future benefits without justification, Moynihan argued that central to the concept of e-government is satisfying expectations by increasing efficiency, effectiveness, openness, participation, and trustworthiness. Moynihan clearly described the same ideas as noted in the article by Thomas and Streib (2005) in trying to define the use of e-democracy, e-commerce, and e-research as categories while questioning the actual process of implementing e-government before determining the potential benefits. Moynihan suggested systems theory as a valid method for analysis of implementation through a mental framework capable of change within systems. By combining the systems theory mental framework suggested by Moynihan with the conceptual framework suggested by Norris and Moon (2005) regarding the sophistication of e-government services, the arguments within the literature enable a clear method for looking at reliability, security, and personal privacy concerns.

Thomas and Streib (2005) argued that the degree of sophistication might be difficult to analyze, given the various stages of e-government capabilities. Questions challenging the potential underutilization and late adoption of sophisticated e-government services change the relationship between the conceptual framework and reliability, security, and personal privacy concerns. If the scholarly literature does not provide a foundation to determine the level of sophistication of e-government services, then additional information is necessary to apply the conceptual framework of sophistication and systems theory. A conceptual framework exists within the literature for evaluation, but that framework does not extend to explicit discussion of reliability, security, and personal privacy concerns. Moynihan (2004) observed that computer security specialists rather than public administrators raise most security and privacy concerns.

Online Methods of Citizen Participation

Beyond e-government are online citizen-participation implementations. Local government implementations of e-commerce, e-research, e-voting, e-governance, e-democracy, and political weblogs all create the possibility of citizen participation. Even citizens' use or lack of use of various implementations provides evidence of citizen participation and preference. For example, Thomas and Streib (2005) looked at the results of a phone survey of Georgia residents to examine the reasons a citizen would access government online, finding that the responses fell into the categories of e-democracy, e-commerce, and e-research. The citizen responses that Thomas and Streib (2005) looked at did not report citizen concerns about reliability, security, and personal privacy, thus limiting discussion on the topic. Thomas and Streib (2005) presented an analysis of future trends and the potential outcomes of e-government, bypassing the resolution of significant process questions about reliability, security, and personal privacy. Public administrators need to move beyond defining the potential benefits of charting a certain course of action to determine best practices. Contemporary public administration literature tends to focus on a specific idea or concept with references to current scholarly articles about e-government. Developing e-government requires a holistic strategy that builds initiatives across all levels of government (Kunstelj & Vintar, 2004).

Researchers traditionally have utilized survey-based rating systems including comparative topic or subject analysis (Poister & Henry, 1994). Public administrator perceptions of citizen preferences could be different from actual citizen preferences (Melkers & Thomas, 1998). Collecting relevant, scholarly e-government literature can be a challenge, given the number of diverse specializations within the field. Articles about e-government exist throughout a multitude of peer-reviewed journals. Reviewing articles or even conducting a meta-analysis of the different arguments and observations advanced in the literature is a necessary first step.

E-Commerce

No discussion of online methods of citizen participation would be complete without an explanation of how e-commerce has changed public expectations about government services. Within the context of e-government, the definition of e-commerce expands to include online financial transactions between government and citizen as well as potential financial transactions between citizens facilitated by the government (Thomas & Streib, 2005). E-commerce will continue to drive e-government services based on increasing citizen expectations for government to provide online alternatives. The successful development of e-government will depend on how well government at all levels can provide services online using contemporary e-commerce capabilities. Public expectations of online services have developed, including service features from paying fines to purchasing a fishing license (Moon, 2002). E-commerce models allow individuals to interact with government online in commercial terms. Traditionally, the business hours of government are the same as the workforce, but traditional business hours create a number of problems for citizens (Fountain, 2001). E-commerce models allow citizens to access services at any time without having limited business hours as a significant barrier and extend the breadth of total services provided.

E-Research

The expansion of e-research is providing citizens with greater online access to information. An open-source methodology exists within current technology movements (Blumenthal, 2005). All of the open-source documents can contribute to e-research. A Markle Foundation (2001) survey showed that a library is the most common metaphor used to describe the Internet. Researchers typically define e-government implementations by the provision of services provided to a community. Providing information to the public is also a government service. Thomas and Streib (2003) examined the results of a telephone survey of why Georgians access government online, determining from the responses that citizens are primarily interested in information about e-democracy, e-commerce, and e-research. According to Thomas and Streib, the concept of e-research involves individuals seeking information independently of the functionality of e-commerce or e-democracy.

E-Voting

Simplified e-voting systems can allow the public to provide input on special projects at the local government level. This type of e-voting allows an online implementation to function as both a record-keeping and record-making system (Barry, 2004). Increasing political apathy and low voter turnout has increased the pressure on governments to provide alternatives to current voting methods. Moynihan (2004) hypothesized that e-voting has an entirely different set of risks than e-government by way of identifying potential dangers of failure for the entire electoral system. For Moynihan, these additional risks clearly establish the difference between e-government and e-voting and suggest that e-government research does not or should not apply directly to e-voting.

E-Governance

Calista and Melitski (2007) indicated that observers of e-government use the word e-governance interchangeably with e-government within the current literature. Streib and Willoughby (2005) considered the current state of e-government implementations in local governments and the potential alternatives available to developing cyber-government. The advent of e-governance inspired technology creates the potential for online forums to provide individuals access to and oversight of the government process. Bovaird (2003) posited that a combination of e-government and e-governance could provide a mechanism for better decision making, data utilization, and general communications. Citizens can demand an increasing degree of interactive e-government services (Streib & Navarro, 2006).

E-Democracy

The expansion of e-democracy initiatives will increase the potential for active civic engagement online. E-democracy allows citizens to communicate preferences online about public issues (Thomas & Streib, 2005). Fountain (2001) focused on debate about information technology having a transformational effect on democracy and civics through the development and explanation of the potential benefits of digital democracy. Arguments about potential benefits depend on a scholar's frame of reference, specifically, different interpretations of technology as a catalyst for institutional change, as a tool for increasing citizen engagement, or as a way to improve current processes within an organization. For instance, political weblogs are challenging previous models of interactions between citizens and elected officials within the framework of representative democracy (Coleman & Wright, 2008). Kerbel and Bloom (2005) commented on the relationship between civic involvement and the online presence of political candidates.

Political Weblogs

Political weblogs provide a unique forum for the study of online methods of citizen participation. As a topic of scholarly discussion, inquiry into political weblogs is only beginning to develop. The nature of journalism and discourse within the public commons has been changing (Hass, 2005). Collaborative problem solving allows a multitude of people to work together toward solving complex problems (Chrislip & Larson, 1994). Weigel (2005) reported the need for observers to follow the trail of money within political weblogs. This logic extends to all large, collaborative projects. Williams, Trammell, Postelnicu, Landreville, and Martin (2005) suggested the use of political weblogs and interconnected hyperlinking enhances a candidate's political campaign. Researchers are starting to move beyond exploratory inquiry toward research utilizing scientific methods of observation. Current political weblog research trends will build the foundation of longitudinal studies. Politicians are notorious for saying different things to different special-interest groups. Weblogs challenge the traditional model of elected officials governing at a distance (Coleman & Moss, 2008). Political weblogs provide a unified platform for citizens interested in political speech or generalized comments intended for a diverse audience.

Political scholarship is entering a digital age (Whitney, 2004). A study of political weblogs requires the scholarly researcher to demonstrate knowledge of specific aspects of organizational leadership. Political weblogs can serve as an active forum for communication with citizens. The methods and strategies employed by politicians within political weblogs demonstrate an inherent relationship to organizational leadership and leadership theory. Trammell, Williams, Postelnicu, and Landreville (2006) described how increasing technical features and interconnectivity are changing candidate websites. Advances in political weblogs will quickly translate to elected officials' expectations of online methods of citizen participation. Political weblogs create a forum for listening (Coleman, 2005).

Electoral campaigns need to maximize limited resources (Varoga, 2005). Political weblogs create a context where complex political communication can remain static. Hanson (2003) evaluated the possibility of town hall meetings or facilitated public dialogues as a democratic teaching tool. Political weblogs can function as perpetual town meetings. The administrative privileges of managing political weblogs create interesting questions for democracy (Perritt, 1997). Websites are devoted to a perpetually increasing number of topics. Even the various political subjects of weblogs raise questions for the consideration of public policy alternatives within the framework of representative democracy (Siapera, 2008). McKenna (2007) defined how policy weblogs could highlight certain issues by presenting highly specialized and limited media coverage. Researchers can examine the technology that allows honest and symbolic exchange within political weblogs (MacDougall, 2005).

Online implementations can transform the expectations and attitudes of participants (West, 2004). Political weblogs provide a forum for elected or campaigning officials to demonstrate organizational leadership potential, creating the foundation for social change. Principles of social change and leadership theory apply to the study of political weblogs. Advanced political weblog techniques include methods of advocating social change and utilizing leadership theory. The tools of social change and leadership theory are evident within political weblog research.

Researchers will advance an argument for building depth within political weblog research. Initial political weblog research can focus on following the money, the relationship with lobbyists, the relationship with political action committees, and the influence of individual donors. Political weblogs can help candidates build e-mail lists. Physical mailings using the postal service are limited financially. Electronic mail campaigns are structurally unlimited (Levey, 2005). The general influence of weblogs on society has changed with the rising popularity of social networking sites and Internet access in general. The providers of any service should consider managing expectations, performance, and satisfaction (Van Ryzin, 2004).

Ethical Considerations

Every individual's perspective adds to the collective knowledge in the scholarly literature on ethical decision making and the administration of information technology. However, some individuals have had a profound impact on how others see the world. Banerjee, Cronan, and Jones (1998) were able to integrate theory and practice in an article about modeling situational ethics within the field of information technology by drawing on a cross section of literature and a series of practical interviews, survey research, and field experience. Public administration is a field that draws on the knowledge of other fields to integrate best practices into the good government model.

Part of the problem with this multidisciplinary focus is that few seminal articles on the subject will use the same references. For example, Foster (1981) posited that a decision maker's awareness of legal and ethical reasons to take action does not guarantee the decision maker will take legal or ethical action. Current articles on the subject do not explicitly reference Foster's observations and from time to time suggest similar conclusions.

Some researchers described extensive methodology, whereas others simply offered explanations of successful practices or case studies of how to correct potential problems by learning from the past. The basis of the study conducted by Banerjee et al. (1998) involved ethical issues surrounding privacy, accuracy, property, and accessibility. Developing solid methodology and successfully reviewing the literature do not guarantee that future issues will not challenge previous assumptions. Some authors examined what technology can do to situational ethics, information technology administration, and organization decision making.

Optimism in this case relies on arguments for increased communication, access, and transparency. For example, e-rulemaking required a concrete definition of various rule-making processes (Noveck, 2004). If e-government, e-rulemaking, and e-democracy can engage individuals normally outside the system, Klinger's (2003) arguments will set the stage for a potentially beneficial future. However, Noveck argued that transparency in e-rulemaking defines the processes associated with the development and implementation of policy. Even with the advent of e-government, e-rulemaking, and e-democracy, changes in technology do not automatically ensure the ethical use of such technology. Conclusions about the future and technological change at this time would be premature, because further research is needed on how transparent and accessible government actually changes information technology administration with respect to ethical decision making. Researchers will have to develop a methodology that will allow looking at special-case scenarios in which individuals and organizations do not act ethically at the individual and organizational levels.

Digital Divide

A certain percentage of the population, particularly based on income, rarely or never has access to the Internet, causing what is caused the digital divide. Narayan (2007) argued that the dispersion of Internet resources remains bimodal, with groupings of extreme access and disenfranchisement through limited access to both e-governance and mobile governance (m-governance, extending e-government to mobile platforms). Within the argument about the nature of access to governmental services online is a series of questions about the potential benefits of government services that are only accessible online (Belanger & Carter, 2009). Kaye (2005) denoted the nature of political weblog users and uses by defining the limited pool of total participants. Providing some government services online requires an online payment system, creating the necessity for an e-commerce methodology for online payment. Some individuals do not have access or only have very limited access to the Internet. Narayan and Nerurkar (2006) previously proposed the possibility of a model for e-governance that could bridge the peripheral access problems of rural areas by providing value proposition and equipping rural areas for access.

Access, Usability, and Trust

Any discussion of e-government should include access, usability, and trust issues associated with feedback collection methods. Polls have suggested that citizens like e-government but have concerns about potential privacy issues (Blair, 2003). Welch, Hinnant, and Moon (2005) concluded that electronic transactions, transparency, and interactivity are all important factors influencing citizen satisfaction with e-government. Tolbert and Mossberger (2006) reported a positive relationship between trust in government and utilizing e-government at local levels. C. N. Davis (2005) suggested the major challenge facing e-government involves accounting for privacy issues while providing access to information.

Technology has allowed a mixture of Internet-driven services and traditional government functions. Australian researchers Dugdale, Daly, Papandrea, and Maley (2005) questioned the potential disconnect between current service demand and potential Internet-driven service users. Questions were also raised regarding how the mixture of Internet-driven services and traditional government is shifting policy concerns from what services to provide to how to connect users to Internet-driven services. Dugdale et al. argued that building online communities to connect socially marginalized communities would require community interest, sustained enthusiasm, and capacity for interaction to realize potential e-government gains in both efficiency and service. Evolution of information technology continues to create ways to manage knowledge within an organization that can help maximize the potential benefits of e-government. Adopting a strategy that requires treating online service users like business clients is part of implementing strategic agency-level approaches during planning, monitoring, and evaluation of e-government.

Discussions of the benefits of civil society rarely denote ways to strengthen it. E-government creates the potential to strengthen civil society (Dugdale et al., 2005). Specifically, Dugdale et al. argued that e-government could strengthen civil society through interactive, online government capabilities that can bring in stakeholders' views, specifically tailored services, and outside interests and experiences, with participation during both the policy design and implementation processes. Risks to civil society include the potential widening of the digital divide in terms of community interests and national interests. Reducing potential risk will require e-government implementations that focus on building collaboration that can overcome access problems due to low availability in rural, remote, or other underserved regions. Collaboration that brings together diverse groups online does not address the initial problem of finding ways to overcome bandwidth supply and availability problems.

Public organizations always should endeavor to look for ways to create value. Finding ways to manage knowledge within an organization can be an avenue to create value. Koh et al. (2005) suggested that an organization could create value by managing knowledge in an e-government consistency model. Technology is changing the course of administrative action and administrative responsibility. Information technology issues create new scenarios that revisit previous ethical considerations. Between previous problems and the development of a new series of potential problems, a gap exists in the current public administration literature. The rate of change creates a moving target for current research. Part of the current trajectory toward the automation of e-government services is by understanding how information technology administrators will answer serious ethical considerations.

Searching the scholarly literature on the subject reveals a series of themes that draw on the relationships among individual action, organizational action, and specific situational considerations that can define action. Researchers can isolate each of these themes in the literature to analyze how public-sector information technology administration occurs in practice. Between globalization pressures and advances in technology, change has triggered the current e-government and e-democracy movement. Changing methods of government service are raising a new set of ethical questions in the field of public administration. Analyzing the scholarly literature on the subject requires a conceptual framework that separates the potential benefit of implementation and the associated externalities. Dealing with potential misuse of information technology requires changes in how organizations gather, store, and maintain sensitive information.

Review of Methods

Within the framework of conducting scholarly research, various academic disciplines provide background information on conducting research (Cooper & Schindler, 2003). McNabb (2002) and Babbie (2004) evaluated the differences between quantitative and qualitative research. Babbie (2002) provided insights into conducting research using quantitative methodologies. Freed, Ryan, and Hess (1991) suggested using a wide variety of statistical methods. Elifson, Runyon, and Haber (1998) defined the basics of statistics within the social sciences. I utilized the Statistical Package for the Social Scientist (SPSS) software to conduct statistical analysis (Norusis, 2002). Hernon (1994) evaluated the role of statistics within the research process, suggesting data analysis can help researcher produce results that can be replicated.

I utilized the mail survey technique to improve the quality of participant results (Mangione, 1995). In terms of conducting a scholarly survey, Cochran (1977) introduced equations for statistical sampling. Information from the academic discipline known as organizational research provides methods for determining the appropriate sample size for a survey (Bartlett, Kotrlik, & Higgins, 2001). Even the best survey research has to avoid participant bias, including biases only visible though extensive questioning (Whitman, 1998). Hunt, Sparkman, and Wilcox (1982) defined the parameters for conducting a pretest to evaluate the survey.

Given the wide range of research methods available to study reliability, security, and personal privacy concerns about e-government implementation, the scholarly literature focuses on only a few methods. Norris and Moon (2005) explained why e-government studies need to adopt a longitudinal perspective, because only longitudinal studies can determine the changing nature of e-government. Norris and Moon described the reliance in the current literature on one-time case studies, interviews, and one-time surveys instead of using longitudinal evaluation methods. For example, West (2004) looked at national public opinion survey data and content analysis, which with revision could include some longitudinal analysis methods. Moynihan (2004) looked at current research and national election statistics, which are an example of longitudinal data, but the application of current research in the article did not include evaluation over time. Norris and Moon (2005) looked at longitudinal evidence from the International City and County Management Association and Public Technology surveys from 2000 and 2002.

Current research in the literature focuses on gathering information about reliability, security, and personal privacy concerns or simply the general practice of identifying problems. After the problem identification stage is complete, the next step in the literature seems on a trajectory to begin evaluation approaches to resolving concerns about reliability, security, and personal privacy. The case study by Ho and Ni (2004) looked at the adoption of e-government features in Iowa, including information security concerns as a factor, but did not include longitudinal elements. Studies that only capture a single cross section of e-government are not going to be able to evaluate change that occurs during the course of implementation.

Summary

This literature review provided an examination of the extent to e-government research methodologies, performance measurement strategies, evaluations of information technology, participation methods, online accessibility, and ethical considerations. Evidence from the literature suggests that at the local government level, different departments coordinate to provide services to citizens, framing the relevant parts of the complex machinery of government. The e-government movement has required the expansion of the machinery of government to facilitate the provision of online services. Authors like Fountain (2001) have argued that the transformational effects of e-government will change government structures. Government functions including e-government services can advance good government values. Throughout the literature, e-government demonstrates that technological change is a phenomenon that influences an equally large domain of knowledge that includes the principles of democratic governance. Several value choices within the field of public administration surround the good government movement's advocacy of increased transparency through civic engagement. Chapter 3 provides details about the research methodology of the study. Chapter 4 provides results, and Chapter 5 concludes the study with recommendations for research and practice.

Chapter 3: Research Method

The academic discipline of philosophy describes the search for knowledge and meaning. Within the broad scope of philosophy, this specific line of research falls within the social sciences (McNabb, 2002). The social sciences represent a body of academic inquiry that includes, but is not limited to, public administration, public policy, and political science (Babbie, 2002). This chapter addresses the research design, sampling, instrumentation, data collection, and ethical considerations. The goal of presenting a quality research methodology, according to McNabb (2002), should be to provide the possibility of replication and predictability. Information presented in this research methods chapter should provide all of the relevant details to replicate the study.

Review of Research Methods of Related Studies

Two studies are closely related to the current research. First, Aikins and Krane (2005) studied a research question related to the deployment of local government resources with respect to administrator preferences or beliefs about citizen participation. The research methods utilized by Aikins and Krane involved evaluating a research question using a cross-sectional survey with a stratified, random sample of local governments with websites. Second, Aikins (2008) studied the presence of deliberative communication features within local government websites with respect to administrator preferences and beliefs about citizen participation. Aikins used research methods involving a cross-sectional, nonexperimental, mixed-methodology design.

Research Questions

This study was designed to determine to what extent the presence of e-feedback mechanisms within local e-government implementations indicates the development of bureaucracy surrounding the information collected using the e-feedback mechanisms. Five research questions guided this study:

1. To what extent do local governments utilize e-government?
2. To what extent do local governments utilize e-feedback?
3. To what extent do local governments audit the information collected from e-feedback implementations?
4. Does a statistically positive relationship exist between the implementation of local e-government services and e-feedback collection methods that increase governmental responsiveness through citizen participation?

5. Does a statistically positive relationship exist between the implementation of local e-feedback mechanisms and auditing functions utilizing the information collected from e-feedback mechanisms?

Research Questions and Outcomes

After a careful review of the prior research relating to e-government within local governments, the results of previous research clearly showed the possibility of implementing e-feedback collection mechanisms. I examined factors related to both the implementation of e-feedback mechanisms and the utilization of e-feedback to collect information to fulfill auditing functions.

Research Hypotheses Related to the Research Questions

Within the framework of conducting academic research, a proposition defines a testable true-or-false statement. Cooper and Schindler (2003) defined a hypothesis as a proposition formulated for empirical testing. Cooper and Schindler suggested a good research hypothesis should be adequate for its purpose, testable, and require few conditions or assumptions. Each research hypothesis involves a strict question without conditional, counter-conditional, or dispositional claims. The following hypotheses and null hypotheses are based on the research questions:

H1. The local government has implemented e-government services.

$H1_0$. The local government has no e-government services implemented.

H2. The local government has implemented e-feedback mechanisms.

$H2_0$. The local government has no e-feedback mechanisms implemented.

H3. The local government uses the information collected from e-feedback mechanisms to fulfill auditing functions.

$H3_0$. The local government does not use information collected from e-feedback mechanisms to fulfill auditing functions.

H4. A statistically positive relationship exists between the implementation of local e-government services and e-feedback collection methods that increase responsiveness through citizen participation.

$H4_0$. No statistically positive relationship exists between the implementation of local e-government services and e-feedback collection methods that increase responsiveness through citizen participation.

H5. A statistically positive relationship exists between the implementation of local e-feedback mechanisms and auditing functions utilizing the information collected from e-feedback mechanisms.

$H5_0$. No statistically positive relationship exists between the implementation of local e-feedback mechanisms and auditing functions utilizing the information collected from e-feedback mechanisms.

After reviewing hypotheses, I reviewed the corresponding data analysis assigned to each research question. Specifically, Table 1 shows each research question, corresponding survey items, and the corresponding data analysis or reporting procedure.

Table 1

Research Questions and Corresponding Data Analysis for Chapter 4

Research question	Corresponding survey item
1. To what extent do local governments utilize e-government?	Items 1–6
2. To what extent do local governments utilize e-feedback?	Items 7–14
3. To what extent do local governments audit the information collected from e-feedback implementations?	Items 15–29
4. Does a statistically positive relationship exist between the implementation of local e-government services and e-feedback collection methods that increase responsiveness through citizen participation?	Items 1–14
5. Does a statistically positive relationship exist between the implementation of local e-feedback mechanisms and auditing functions utilizing the information collected from e-feedback mechanisms?	Items 7–29

Operational Variable

This research relied on a number of operational variables. These operational variables were a necessary part of the research design. The research design included a traditionally derived framework for the study that involved a set of operational variables:

43

dependent variables, independent variables, and control variables (see Table 2).

Table 2

Operational Variables

Dependent variable	Independent variables	Control variables
Implementation of e-government, as evidenced by the following: • Online access to services • Online records requests • Online permitting • Online payments • Online contact information	1. Implementation of e-feedback, as evidenced by the following: • Online surveys • Online polling • Virtual focus groups • E-mail surveys • Automated phone surveys • Tracking website statistics • E-government benchmarks 2. Auditing e-feedback, as evidenced by the following: • General auditing functions • Auditing citizen interaction • Auditing decision making • Auditing strategic planning • Budget auditing • Auditing workforce • Auditing automation • Independent auditing • Internal staff evaluation • Optimization modeling • Numerical modeling • Improving e-government • Expanding e-government • Developing public policy	Local governments without elements of e-government were excluded from the study.

Dependent Variables

The study depended on the presence of e-government implementations within local government. The study tested the dependent variable with both direct and indirect questions. With respect to a direct test of the dependent variable, a question measured the implementation of e-government. Indirectly to test the implementation of e-government, several variables were investigated, including online access to services, online records requests, online permitting, online payments, and online contact information.

Independent Variables

The independent variable in this case involved identifying e-feedback mechanisms within local governments with e-government implementations. The study identified the presence of e-feedback and determined how local governments use information collected from e-feedback for auditing purposes.

The study of independent variables included both direct and indirect analyses. In terms of direct analysis of the independent variables, one of the questions directly tested the implementation of e-feedback. Indirect study of the degree of e-feedback implementation included the variables of online surveys, online polling, virtual focus groups, e-mail surveys, automated phone surveys, website statistics, and e-government benchmarks.

A second set of independent variables included a direct question about auditing e-feedback. The second group of variables observed indirectly included general auditing functions, auditing citizen interaction, auditing decision making, auditing strategic planning, budget auditing, auditing workforce, auditing automation, independent auditing, internal staff evaluation, optimization modeling, numerical modeling, improved e-government, expanded e-government, and development of public policy.

Control Variables

This study controlled for local governments without any implemented e-government. Exclusion of each government without any implemented e-government helped define the total universe of the study.

Research Design

Research methods used in this study followed a sequence of steps described within the quantitative tradition of inquiry (McNabb, 2002). Three types of quantitative designs are available to social scientists for conducting research: (a) exploratory designs, (b) descriptive designs, and (c) causal designs (McNabb, 2002). The scope of the systemic questions about e-government feedback methodologies involved in the study precluded the pilot study style of an exploratory design. A causal-design study based on experimentation would require extensive access to individuals involved in e-government throughout the United States (McNabb, 2002). A descriptive-design study is congruent with the survey format, excluding the possibility of both the exploratory and causal designs.

This study used a quantitative-based, descriptive field survey to collect information from a defined population (McNabb, 2002). Surveys allow researchers to study large populations without direct observations (Babbie, 2004). A field survey involving a self-administered questionnaire is the best way to define the current state of a phenomenon like e-feedback collection methods and e-government services (McNabb, 2002). A matrix question format allowed the participant to answer several questions with the same potential responses (Babbie, 2002). The survey design used the semantic differential scale to allow the participant to identify difference between two extremes on a 7-point scale (McNabb, 2002).

Other potential research designs are available to researchers, including quantitative and combined (mixed model). All three traditions of inquiry received consideration. This study utilized the quantitative tradition. Qualitative research designs include explanatory, interpretive, and critical (McNabb, 2002). The qualitative explanatory research design attempts to provide a combination of meaning and description (McNabb, 2002).

Evaluating meaning and description at the same time presents significant challenges to evaluating e-feedback collection methodologies. Qualitative, interpretative research design evaluates meaning in terms of circumstance, event, or social situation (McNabb, 2002). Without a detailed study of e-feedback methodologies, critical research would be premature. Within the field of public administration, researchers can collect qualitative data by observation, participation, interviews, and document analysis (McNabb, 2002). Direct access to a wide variety of cities would preclude observation, participation, and interviewing. The availability of e-government documents for analysis created a barrier to qualitative data collection by document analysis.

Combination (mixed-model) research designs bring together elements from quantitative and qualitative designs in the form of archival, media, and artifact studies (McNabb, 2002). Archival combination designs utilize historical documents, and media combination designs utilize current documents (McNabb, 2002). The availability of e-government documents developed and disseminated by local governments precludes the potential utilization of archival and media data collection methods. Artifact studies are traditionally only germane when applying methods from the field of archaeology to social science questions (McNabb, 2002). During the initial development phase of e-government services, data collection for artifact studies would be extremely limited.

Setting and Sample

The study setting involves current e-government implementations. Specifically, this study involved e-feedback collection methods inside current e-government implementations within local governments in the United States. Description of the study setting and sample includes sample characteristics, study population, sampling method, sample size, and the participants' eligibility criteria.

Sample Characteristics

Characteristics of the selected sample included elements defining the principle city of the metropolitan and micropolitan statistical areas. Each principle city had similar characteristics defined by the U.S. Census. The size of the sample had a direct relationship to the representative nature of the sample. Comparing population or budget characteristics of the selected sample provided evidence of the representative nature of the sample.

Study Population

The study population concept also describes the sampling universe. The study population in this case described the total number of eligible participants. The Office of Management and Budget (2008) identified a list of 953 metropolitan and micropolitan statistical areas in the United States (OMB Bulletin No. 09-01). Using the metropolitan and micropolitan statistical areas provided a defined sampling universe that represented the largest potential interaction between citizens and government online. This target audience defined the current state of e-feedback collection methods and e-government services within cities in the United States. Limiting the survey to the metropolitan and micropolitan statistical areas helped provide a defined and manageable sample.

Sampling Method

Sampling methods that received consideration for use within this study included systemic sampling, stratified sampling, and probability proportionate to size sampling. Systemic sampling evaluates elements in a list by a defined sampling interval, which in this study would be excluded due to the creation of an alphabetical, population, or budget bias (McNabb, 2002). Stratified sampling involves sampling based on relatively homogeneous grouping, which in this study would require developing a defined population or budget bias resulting in the exclusion of this method from consideration (Babbie, 2004). Probability proportionate to size sampling involves selecting a fixed number of elements from defined clusters, which in this study would require intentionally introducing a grouping bias (McNabb, 2002).

Based on the previously enumerated sampling methods, the method used to select potential participants from the available sampling universe was simple random sampling. Mangione (1995) listed several potential pitfalls of sampling, including list reliability, coverage biases, selection bias, responsiveness, and weighting nonparticipants. Within a simple random sample, each potential participant has an equal chance of participation in the probability-based study (McNabb, 2002). A defined sampling universe makes nonprobability sampling methods unnecessary (Babbie, 2002). A representative, simple, random sample allows the potential for inference to the sampling universe.

A sampling frame defines the criteria for defining the limits of a probability sample (Babbie, 2002). The sampling frame for this study included a list of the primary metropolitan statistical areas that included U.S. cities with the largest populations. Sampling involved a computer-based, random-number generator program. The computer-based, random-number generator produced a list of randomly generated unique numbers, reducing the potential for bias and allowing the potential for inference to the sampling universe.

Sample Size

Sample size defines the number of participants selected from the sampling universe. The sampling universe included 953 metropolitan and micropolitan statistical areas in the United States. Calculating the sample size involved estimating the acceptable rate of standard error. Bartlett, Kotrlik, and Higgins (2001) suggested that sample size in survey research should be determined by using Cochran's (1977) sample-size formula for continuous data:

$$\underline{n}_0 = \frac{(\underline{t})^2 * (\underline{s})^2}{(\underline{d})^2} = \frac{(1.96)^2 (1.167)^2}{(7 * .03)^2} = 118. \qquad (1)$$

A sample size of 118 would be larger than 5% of the total sampling universe, requiring Cochran's (1977) correction formula:

$$\underline{n} = \frac{\underline{n}_0}{(1 + \underline{n}_0 / Population} = \frac{(118)}{(1 + 118 / 953)} = 105. \qquad (2)$$

In order to ensure reliable results, Salkind (1997) suggested oversampling by 40% or 50%. Within this study, a modification of

Cochran's (1977) correction formula involved a 50% increase in total sample size:

$$n = \frac{n_0}{(1 + n_0 / Population)} * 1.5 = \frac{(118)}{(1 + 118/953)} * 1.5 = 157.5. \quad (3)$$

The simple random sample included 158 metropolitan and micropolitan statistical areas in the United States. A sampling ratio represented the sample size divided by the sampling universe, or 158/953 (Babbie, 2002). Oversampling resulted in the sample size representing 16% of the total sampling universe.

Participant Eligibility Criteria

The expected participants were each city manager. If the city did not have a city manager, the mayor was the expected participant. A consistent sampling method helped ensure the survey reached a consistent level within the organization (McNabb, 2002). The survey instructions specified the city manager as the intended participant, but delegation of the survey remained a possibility. Achieving a high response rate was dependent on each participant's willingness to participate in the study.

A random sample of principle cities that represented the primary metropolitan statistical areas received surveys. Study participation eligibility criteria included determining if the principle city in question was included in the 953 metropolitan and micropolitan statistical areas sampling universe. In addition to being a part of the sampling universe, the participant also had to work within the principle city of the metropolitan and micropolitan statistical area.

Survey Instrument

The materials associated with the survey instrumentation facilitate a researcher conducting a study. A standard survey instrument helped disseminate the questions to multiple participants. Variability would result from the preferences of the participant, not the survey instrumentation. Explanation of the study survey instrumentation and materials involves describing the type of survey instrument, survey procedures, reliability, validity, bias, and survey completion.

Type of Survey Instrument

The field survey instrument included a self-administered questionnaire delivered by the U.S. Postal Service. A letter attached to the survey provided instructions for completing the questionnaire (McNabb, 2002). Questions within the field survey were formulated to involve closed-ended questions that listed potential options for the participant (Babbie, 2002). The survey structure began with general questions about the form of government and the size of the city's information technology department. After the general-questions section, three independent-variable sections and one dependent-variable section completed the survey.

Survey Procedures

The participants received a self-administered mail survey. The research procedure included a major mail survey, 2-week follow-up, 1-month follow-up, and finally a 2-month follow-up. Mail distribution involved a computer-generated address and return label placed on a standard-sized envelope. The local office of the U.S. Postal Service received all of the initial survey questionnaires at the same time. Each envelope contained a self-addressed, stamped return envelope; introductory letter; and survey questionnaire. Returned self-administered questionnaires were monitored and recorded. Two graphs were generated illustrating daily returns and the total percentage of returns (Babbie, 2004). Follow-up mailings occurred based on the return-monitoring process at 2 weeks, 1 month, and finally at 2 months. Each follow-up survey questionnaire envelope included a follow-up letter; a self-addressed, stamped return envelope; introductory letter; and survey questionnaire. Coded data from returned survey questionnaires were stored in a basic tab-delineated computer database.

Survey Reliability

This section discusses the reliability of the instrument development, internal survey consistency, and experimental replication. In order to ensure study reliability, all of the participants received the same survey instrument and materials. Distributing the same survey instrument and materials to all participants created a degree of uniformity and reliability. Outside the potential actions of the research, the survey participants needed to be reliable (Babbie, 2004). Sampling city managers provided a pool of professional and reliable participants. Not only would the sample reliability increase with a bigger sample size, but also the destructive nature of the survey process would increase (McNabb, 2002).

Every survey involves a development process that takes into account reliability questions. Each question in the survey was brief, relevant, and clearly related to the study of e-government (McNabb, 2002). A limit of 50 words controlled the potential length of each question or instructional paragraph. All of the survey questions evaluated participant preference without the introduction of negative phrasing (Babbie, 2002). The number of variables involved in the study necessitated the introduction of questions involving a matrix format.

Survey Validity

A study needs to have a high degree of both reliability and validity (Babbie, 2002). Survey validity defines how accurately participant preferences are measured by the survey instrument. The artificial nature of survey research historically presents stronger reliability than validity (Babbie, 2002). Participant preferences are complex. In order to model participant preferences, the question design included a matrix format utilizing a 7-point semantic differential scale. Researchers have to acknowledge this limitation of survey research. Quantitative analysis of preferences requires coding schemes that inherently limit the scope of potential responses.

Survey Bias

Surveys inherently have a destructive nature, because participants might begin to think about the questions. Forms of potential bias include intentional false positives, optimism gaps, and individual differences in perspective. All participant data provide only an approximation of preferences. A significant number of participants refusing to answer survey questions creates nonresponse error (McNabb, 2002). Response distortion occurs when the survey questions are poorly structured. The sampling universe included 953 metropolitan and micropolitan statistical areas in the United States, reducing the potential for sampling error or non-sampling error by standardizing potential participants. McNabb (2002) defined data error in terms of distortions in the dataset made from coding irregularities or researcher mistakes.

Survey Completion

Completing the survey instrument required a number of processes. Participants needed to receive the self-administered mail survey. Participants needed to complete the survey after reading the introductory letter. Each participant should have answered all of the questions. After completing the survey, participants needed to return the survey in the self-addressed, stamped return envelope to the U.S. Postal Service.

Concepts Measured by the Survey

This study used three groups of variables presented in matrix question format: (a) e-government service implementation, (b) e-feedback collection methods, and (c) e-feedback auditing (Figure 2). Each question sampled the participant's perception about current implementation and future implementation.

Figure 2. Measured elements.

Question 1. Does the local government utilize e-government? The first section of the survey evaluated the participant's perception of e-government service implementation. A matrix style question asked the participant,

> The following question addresses the implementation of e-government services. Generally, e-government describes the provision of services for citizens online. From your personal experiences and knowledge, rate the degree of implementation for the following potential e-government services in your city both now and the degree of implementation based on any planned future expansion from 1, not implemented, to 7, fully implemented.

This question included a large number of potential local government services. Specific services in the matrix format question included online access to services, online records requests, online permitting, online contact information, online payments, and automated online services.

Question 2. Does the local government utilize e-feedback? The second section of the survey helped catalog the implementation of e-feedback collection methods. A matrix style question asked the participant,

> The following question addresses the implementation of e-feedback. Conceptually, e-feedback describes various forms of online interaction with citizens for the purposes of collecting information. From your personal experiences and knowledge, rate the current implementation of the following e-feedback collection mechanisms in your city both now and the degree of implementation based on any planned future expansion from 1, being not implemented, to 7, being fully implemented.

Specific feedback collection methods in the matrix format question included online surveys, online polling, virtual focus groups, e-mail surveys, automated phone surveys, tracking website statistics, and e-government benchmarks.

Question 3. Does the local government audit the information collected from within e-feedback implementations? The third section of the survey helped catalog the participant's perception of e-feedback usage. A matrix style question asked the participant,

The following question attempts to evaluate what local governments are doing with the information collected from e-feedback implementations. From your personal experiences and knowledge, rate the use of e-feedback data (e.g., from online surveys, online polling, virtual focus groups, or e-mail surveys) in your city both now and the degree of implementation based on any planned future expansion, from 1, being not implemented, to 7, being fully implemented.

Specific organizational e-feedback usage methods in the matrix format question included improving e-government, process automation, numerical modeling, initiating citizen interaction, community outreach projects, setting budget priorities, administrative decisions, organizational decisions, internal staff evaluation, independent auditing, developing public policy, and expanding e-government.

Data Availability

A complete listing of all raw data from the study was not directly included in the dissertation. Presentation of relevant processed data involved tables or graphs presented throughout the results and conclusions chapters.

Survey Testing Method

During the course of the research project, testing the survey questionnaire helped reduce the possibility of error by identifying questions that were impossible for the participant to answer (Babbie, 2002). Expert review is a method of testing the survey. Potential differences in language precluded the use of expert review for the survey testing method. The survey pretest needed several participants to ensure the language within the survey was clear. McNabb (2002) suggested the best method for testing the survey questionnaire involves administering the survey to a small random sample. Hunt, Sparkman, and Wilcox (1982) suggested the size of the pretest survey sample should be relatively small, but the exact size is variable relative to the specific survey instrument.

Determination of a small, pretest sample size involved modifying Cochran's (1977) sample-size formula for continuous data. This study used a modification of Cochran's (1977) correction formula by increasing the total sample size by 50%. The previously calculated sample size of 158 requires a 10% adjustment for pretesting:

$$\underline{n} = \left(\frac{\underline{n}_0}{(1 + \underline{n}_0 / Population} * 1.5 \right) * .10 = \left(\frac{(118)}{(1 + 118 / 953)} * 1.5 \right) * .10$$

$$= 15.75.$$

(4)

The pretesting phase of the survey development involved sending out 16 surveys. The pretesting sample size defined the number of participants selected from the sampling universe. Within this study the sampling universe included 953 metropolitan and micropolitan statistical areas in the United States.

Data Collection

The data collection process occurred after participants received the self-administered mail survey. Following the previously established research procedure, each envelope contained a self-addressed, stamped return envelope; introductory letter; and survey questionnaire. The data collection process involved monitoring and recording the returned self-administered questionnaires. Two graphs were generated illustrating daily returns and the total percentage of returns (Babbie, 2004). The U.S. Postal Service distributed all of the questionnaires at the same time. Participants' return dates for the questionnaires were variable. Using the SPSS data-editor capability enabled the manual entry of information into the data-editor window (McNabb, 2002). Coded data from returned survey questionnaires were stored in an SPSS Save File based on a tab-delineated computer database. See Table 3 for the specific data inventory.

Table 3

Participant Survey-Item Inventory and Data Format

Module	Item
Descriptive information	Population
	Form of government
	Survey response time
E-government	Online access to services
	Online records requests
	Online permitting
	Online contact information
	Online payments
	Automated online services
E-feedback module	Online surveys
	Online polling
	Virtual focus groups
	E-mail surveys
	Automated phone surveys
	Tracking website statistics
	E-government benchmarks
E-feedback usage	Improving e-government
	Process automation
	Numerical modeling
	Initiating citizen interactions
	Community outreach projects
	Setting budget priorities
	Administrative decisions
	Organizational decisions
	Strategic planning
	Internal staff evaluation
	Independent auditing
	Developing public policy
	Expanding e-government

Survey Data From the Census of Government

Each of the randomly selected local governments had certain information available within the Census of Government. For example, the survey instrument did not need to collect information about the form of government, total population, budget, or population demographics. This descriptive statistical information is currently publicly available and did not require collection through the deployment of a survey instrument.

Local Government Grouping Protocol

With the survey universe, a grouping protocol involved categorizing each of the randomly selected local governments by population. A separation of the metropolitan statistical areas and micropolitan statistical areas enhanced the relevance of the statistical analysis conducted utilizing the survey results.

Statistical Analysis

I conducted all of the statistical analyses. The study did not require retaining the services of a professional statistician. The computer software used during the data analysis portion of the study was the September 9, 2000, release version 10.1.0 of the SPSS Standard Version. A philosophy for applying statistical analysis is necessary to ensure consistency. Each variable received a degree of statistical analysis. Varieties of mechanisms for statistical analysis provided additional data description.

The process of statistical analysis began with each variable receiving statistical analysis based on response counts. After computing response counts, several statistical mechanisms helped compute descriptive statistics. Statistics can describe data by summarizing the mode, median, and arithmetic average. Analysis included a comparison of the means and median for each variable. Additional statistical analysis involved looking at variability measures including range, variance, standard deviation, and coefficient of variation.

Beyond the basic descriptive statistical analysis, additional statistical mechanisms deployment included variable group comparison, distribution evaluation, combination variables, sample size effect, binomial tests, and normal distribution tests. McNabb (2002) discussed four analytic processes that utilize SPSS: (a) descriptive statistics, (b) graphical displays, (c) data modification, and (d) inferential statistical analysis. Statistics helped review the relationships between the variable groups. All variables included in the study received descriptive and frequency statistical analyses, including mean, median, mode, standard deviation, variance, range, minimum, maximum, standard error of the mean, skewness, and kurtosis. A review of the basic descriptive and frequency statistical analysis tests provided a general understanding of participant preferences to support the selection of graphical displays (see Table 4).

Table 4

Variable Names for Statistical Analysis

Module and item	Statistical analysis
Descriptive information	
Population	POP
Form of government	FOG
Survey response time	SRT
E-government	
Online access to services	Services
Online records requests	Requests
Online permitting	Permits
Online contact information	Contact
Online payments	Payments
Automated online services	Automated
E-feedback module	
Online surveys	Surveys
Online polling	Polling
Virtual focus groups	Groups
E-mail surveys	Email
Automated phone surveys	Phone
Tracking website statistics	Website
E-government benchmarks	Benchmarks
E-feedback usage	
Improving e-government	Improving
Process automation	Process
Numerical modeling	Modeling
Initiating citizen interactions	Citizens
Community outreach projects	Outreach
Setting budget priorities	Budget
Administrative decisions	Admin
Organizational decisions	Org
Strategic planning	Strategy
Internal staff evaluation	Internal
Independent auditing	Auditing
Developing public policy	Policy
Expanding e-government	Expanding

Data Analysis for Research Questions 1–3

The first research question investigated to what extent local governments utilized e-government. In order to test this conjecture, a matrix style question from the mail survey stated,

57

The following question addresses the implementation of e-government services. Generally, e-government describes the provision of services for citizens online. From your personal experiences and knowledge, rate the degree of implementation for the following potential e-government services in your city both now and the degree of implementation based on any planned future expansion from 1, not implemented to 7, fully implemented.

Specifically, the matrix style question included the following items: e-government, online access to services, online records requests, online permitting, online payments, and online contract information. Each of the items measured received descriptive and frequency statistical analyses. The specific tests for each item included mean, median, mode, standard deviation, variance, range, minimum, maximum, standard error of the mean, skewness, and kurtosis.

The second research question investigated to what extent local governments utilized e-feedback. In order to test this conjecture, a matrix style question from the mail survey stated,

The following question addresses the implementation of e-feedback. Conceptually, e-feedback describes various forms of online interaction with citizens for the purposes of collecting information. From your personal experiences and knowledge, rate the current implementation of the following e-feedback collection mechanisms in your city both now and the degree of implementation based on any planned future expansion from 1, being not implemented, to 7, being fully implemented.

Specifically, the matrix style question included the following items: e-feedback, online surveys, online polling, virtual focus groups, e-mail surveys, automated phone surveys, tracking website statistics, and e-government benchmarks. Each of the items measured received descriptive and frequency statistical analyses. The specific tests for each item included mean, median, mode, standard deviation, variance, range, minimum, maximum, standard error of the mean, skewness, and kurtosis.

The third research question investigated to what extent local governments audited the information collected from e-feedback implementations. In order to test this conjecture, a matrix style question from the mail survey stated,

The following question attempts to evaluate what local governments are doing to audit the information collected from e-feedback implementations. From your personal experiences and knowledge within local government, rate the auditing of e-feedback data (e.g., from online surveys, online polling, virtual focus groups, or e-mail surveys) in your city both now and the degree of implementation based on any planned future expansion from 1, being not implemented, to 7, being fully implemented.

Specifically, the matrix style question included the following items: auditing e-feedback, general auditing functions, auditing decision making, auditing strategic planning, budget auditing, auditing workforce, auditing automation, independent auditing, internal staff evaluation, optimization modeling, improving e-government, expanding e-government, and developing public policy. Each of the items measured received descriptive and frequency statistical analyses. The specific tests for each item included mean, median, mode, standard deviation, variance, range, minimum, maximum, standard error of the mean, skewness, and kurtosis.

Justification for and limitations of statistical analysis. The information collected from the matrix style question advanced the research by using enumerated weighted preferences to define the degree of implementation for e-government, e-feedback, and auditing e-feedback. Understanding the relationship between e-government, e-feedback, and auditing e-feedback within local government required measuring each element individually. However, by definition, statistical analysis involves limits. Before the study began, limits existed based on the total universe represented within the study. The total number of local governments within the United States limited the size of the sampling frame and thus limited the statistical analysis. After defining the sampling universe, the participant response rate limited the analysis. The scale used within the survey questions also limited the potential responses from 1–7. In addition to the structural limits associated with the size and scope of the survey universe, the survey format limited the modes of preference discovery within a quantitative survey.

Possible outcomes. The format of the question influenced the potential responses from 1 (not implemented) to 7 (fully implemented). Potential outcomes for the research question included a measurable degree of implementation. The results defined an outcome between not being implemented to being fully implemented.

Data Analysis for Research Question 4

The fourth research question involved a testable conjecture: Does a statistically positive relationship exist between the implementation of local e-government services and e-feedback collection methods that increase governmental responsiveness through citizen participation? Two bivariate correlation tests were performed for this research question. First, a bivariate correlation test of the degree of implementation of e-government services as a composite variable and the degree of implementation of e-feedback collection methods as a composite variable was conducted using the SPSS software package. Second, a bivariate correlation test of the degree of implementation of e-government services and the degree of implementation of e-feedback collection methods was conducted.

The bivariate correlation testing provided a statistical method to compare e-government implementation with e-feedback implementation. By definition, statistical analysis involves limits. Before the study began, limits existed based on the total universe represented within the study. The total number of local governments within the United States limited the size of the sampling frame and thus limited the statistical analysis. After the sampling universe was defined, the participant response rate limited the analysis. The scale used within the survey questions also limited the potential responses from 1–7. In addition to the structural limits associated with the size and scope of the survey universe, the survey format limited the modes of preference discovery within a quantitative survey. The potential outcomes from the bivariate correlation test would provide evidence about the relationship between e-government implementation and e-feedback implementation.

Data Analysis for Research Question 5

The fifth research question involved a testable conjecture: Does a statistically positive relationship exist between the implementation of local e-feedback mechanisms and auditing functions utilizing the information collected from e-feedback mechanisms? Two bivariate correlation tests were performed for this research question. First, a bivariate correlation test of the degree of implementation of e-feedback services as a composite variable and the degree of implementation of auditing e-feedback collection methods as a composite variable was conducted using the SPSS software package. Second, a bivariate correlation test of the degree of implementation of e-feedback services and the degree of implementation of auditing using e-feedback methods was conducted.

The bivariate correlation testing provided a statistical method to compare e-feedback implementation with e-feedback auditing implementation. By definition, statistical analysis involves limits. Before the study began, limits existed based on the total universe represented within the study. The total number of local governments within the United States limited the size of the sampling frame. After the sampling universe received definition, the participant response rate limited the analysis. The scale used within the survey questions also limited the potential responses from 1–7. In addition to the structural limits associated with the size and scope of the survey universe, the survey format limited the modes of preference discovery within a quantitative survey. The potential outcomes from the bivariate correlation test provided evidence about the relationship between e-feedback implementation and e-feedback auditing implementation.

Findings Presentation

After I conducted the study and collected and analyzed data, the process of building a presentation began (McNabb, 2002). A definitive point of view can help guide the presentation of findings (McNabb, 2002). The findings presentation began with two distinct points of view. First, the analytical organization point of view allowed the study to address research questions directly. Second, after addressing each research question separately, the comparative-pattern point of view helped illustrate relationships between the groups of questions in the survey questionnaire. After the conclusion of the research project, each research question required a degree of fine-tuning to determine if the question was appropriate or if an alternative question existed (Cooper & Schindler, 2003).

Ethical Protection of Participants

Several measures served to protect study participant's rights. All participants had absolute anonymity. The Walden University Institutional Review Board reviewed and approved the research study before the collection or analysis of any data. The Institutional Review Board would have received all adverse event-reporting forms about questionnaire events, discrete or general, within a week, which would have provided a degree of institutional oversight.

Chapter Summary

The research method chapter introduced how the research design involved a quantitative, descriptive field survey to collect information not available in current research studies. The study statistical analysis included descriptive measures and correlation tests. A field survey involving a self-administered questionnaire documented the current state of e-feedback collection methods and e-government services. Survey instrumentation included questions in a matrix format and a 7-point semantic differential scale. Chapter 4 provides results, and Chapter 5 concludes the study with recommendations for research and practice.

Chapter 4: Results

I addressed the formation of bureaucratic structures around e-feedback. The principle investigation of the study was accomplished by evaluating the overarching research question: To what extent does the presence of e-feedback mechanisms within local e-government implementations indicate the development of bureaucracy based on such e-feedback? Five specific research questions were formulated to answer the overarching question of the study:

1. To what extent do local governments utilize e-government?

2. To what extent do local governments utilize e-feedback?

3. To what extent do local governments audit the information collected from e-feedback implementations?

4. Does a statistically significant, positive relationship exist between the implementation of local e-government services and e-feedback collection methods that increase governmental responsiveness through citizen participation?

5. Does a statistically significant, positive relationship exist between the implementation of local e-feedback mechanisms and auditing functions utilizing the information collected from e-feedback mechanisms?

Overview of the Chapter

Information presented within chapter 4 used the following framework to explain and define the results identified from the collection of survey data during the study:

1. Procedural survey notes were provided to ensure full disclosure of all relevant aspects of the research methodology implementation. Reporting was provided to explain how the standard Walden University ethical protections were used during the study to protect the participants.

2. The survey response rate was analyzed and explained.

3. An explanation was included of all the steps taken to adhere to the findings presentation guidelines defined in chapter 3.

4. The results of each research question were provided with relevant charts and graphs.

5. A summary section concluded the results chapter.

Procedural Survey Notes

I sent 16 pretest surveys and 158 surveys via the U.S. Postal Service; a total of three letters were returned without postage (the stamps might have fallen off during the handling process), and three were returned with an invalid address error. Addresses were identified using the Census of Government database. Based on the survey process, all of the measures designed to protect the study participant's rights were followed during the deployment and execution phase of the research project. The anonymity of all participants who participated in the study remains intact. All of the survey questionnaire envelopes have been shredded, and the questionnaires will remain sealed within a safe deposit box for 10 years after the study. The Walden University Institutional Review Board completed a review and approved the research study before the collection or analysis of any data. Walden University's approval number for this study is 02-25-10-0297683, and it expired February 24, 2011. The entire survey deployment and recovery process was complete before the expiration of the Institutional Review Board timeline. During the course of conducting the study, no adverse event-reporting forms about questionnaire events, discrete or general, were reported to the Institutional Review Board for institutional oversight.

Survey Response Rate

The survey had a relatively strong response rate for a mail survey of local governments located within the United States (McNabb, 2002). The study included a total sampling frame of 174, with 41 returned survey instruments for a total response rate of 23.56%:

$$\underline{n} = \frac{R_1}{(S_1 + S_2)} = \frac{(41)}{(158 + 16)} = 23.56\%. \tag{5}$$

Overall the response rate for the study was slightly lower than expected, but the total number or percentage of surveys returned for the study was above the 17% threshold necessary to complete statistical analysis based on normal distributions.

Adhering to the Findings Presentation

Adhering to the findings presentation outlined in Chapter 3 required direct reporting of the facts within Chapter 4. All conclusions were strictly limited to chapter 5. The findings presentation begins with two distinct points of view. First, the analytical organization point of view allowed the study to address the results of each research question directly. Second, after addressing each research question separately, the comparative-pattern point of view helped the contents of Chapter 5 illustrate existing relationships between the groups of questions in the survey questionnaire. Finally, within Chapter 5 (the conclusion of the research project) each research question required a degree of fine-tuning to determine if the question was appropriate or if an alternative question existed (Cooper & Schindler, 2003).

Research Question 1 Results

To what extent do local governments utilize e-government? In order to better examine a collection of elements that describe e-government, a series of survey questions asked participants about online access to services, online records requests, online permitting, online payments, and online contact information, both now and in the future (Tables 5–8). This set of variables had a very low missing N value compared to the rest of the survey questions. When the participants were asked about e-government as a variable, 36 answered the question about e-government now, with five declining to provide any answer. One of the trends within the results involved a larger number of participants answering questions about now compared to answers about the future. Specifically, in the case of the future e-government variable the participants answered 33 times and declined to answer the question eight times. As a group the mean response for current e-government utilization was 3.36, based on a scale of 1 (not utilized or implemented) to 7 (fully utilized or implemented). The intended future utilization of e-government was higher than the current utilization, with a mean response of 5.06 for the survey question (Table 5). Beyond the general descriptive analysis of the e-government research question, several elements provided symptomatic evidence of e-government within a local government online environment, including online access to services, online records requests, online permitting, online payments, and online contact information.

Table 5

Descriptive Analysis of the E-Government Variable (Now and Future)

Statistic	E-government now	E-government in the future
N		
Valid	36	33
Missing	5	8
Mean	3.36	5.06
Std. error of mean	0.27	0.25
Median	3.00	5.00
Mode	3.00	5.00[a]
Std. deviation	1.62	1.43
Variance	2.64	2.06
Skewness	0.56	-0.32

Kurtosis	-0.21	-0.85
Range	6.00	5.00
Minimum	1.00	2.00
Maximum	7.00	7.00
Sum	121.00	167.00

Note. Based on a scale of 1 (*not implemented*) to 7 (*fully implemented*).
[a] Multiple modes exist. The smallest value is shown.

All of the survey responses by the participants to the direct e-government (now) question represented a relatively normal distribution. Based on a purely normal curve, the mean would be at 3.50, compared to the actual mean of 3.36 (Figure 3). The distribution illustrated a utilization of the full response range by the participants between 1 and 7.

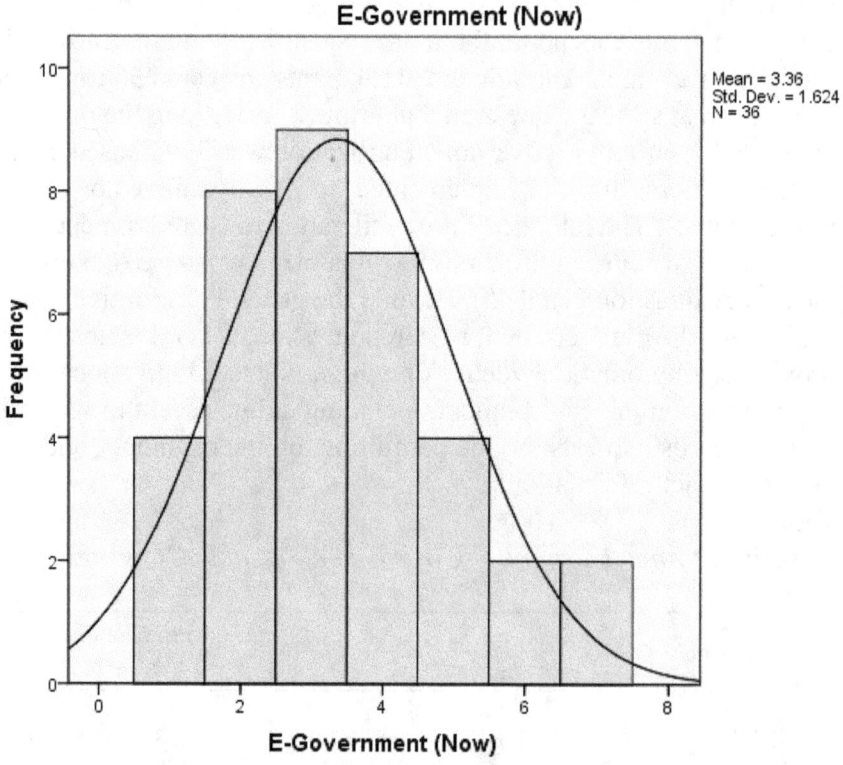

Figure 3. Histogram of e-government (now).
After reviewing e-government (now) as a variable, a histogram of e-government future illustrated an upward shift in the overall data returned by the participants (Figure 4). The mean of 5.06 showed an increase over the e-government (now) at 3.36 (as shown in Figure 3). Comparing histograms provides one of the best methods to visually compare the two sets of data.

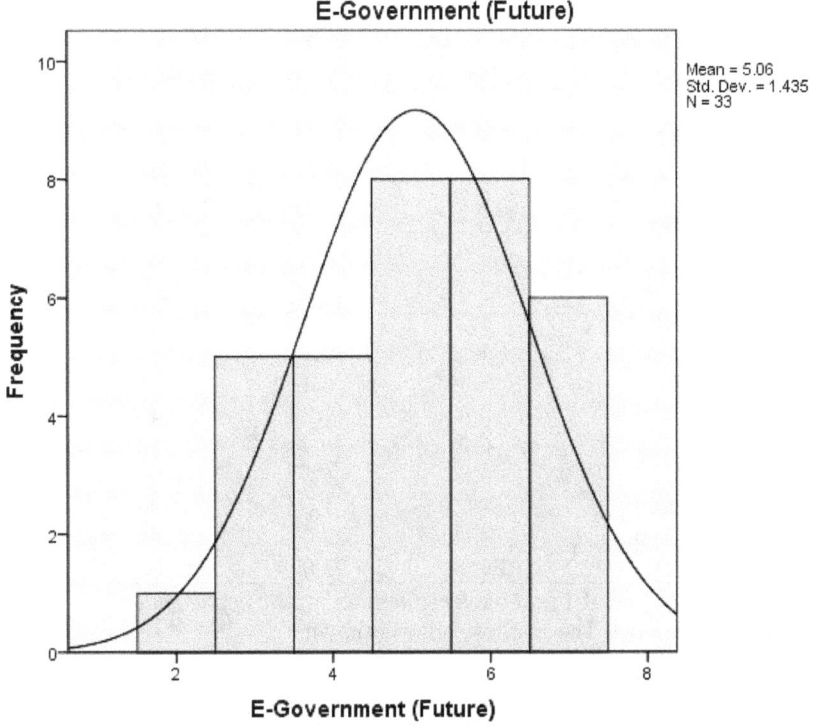

Figure 4. Histogram of e-government (future).

A separate question was devised in order to better understand the perceptions of ways that local governments will utilize the e-government factors in the future. Participants were asked to define the current utilization of all of the factors: online access to services, online records requests, online permitting, online payments, and online contact information (Table 6). The specific tests for each item included mean, median, mode, standard deviation, variance, range, minimum, maximum, standard error of the mean, skewness, and kurtosis.

Table 6

Descriptive Analysis of E-Government Utilization Variables (Now)

Statistic	Online access to services	Online records requests	Online permitting	Online payments	Online contact information
N					
Valid	37	39	38	37	38
Missing	4	2	3	4	3
Mean	3.49	2.79	2.45	3.05	5.76
Std. error of mean	0.27	0.32	0.34	0.35	0.26
Median	3.00	2.00	1.00	3.00	6.00
Mode	2.00[a]	1.00	1.00	1.00	7.00
Std. deviation	1.66	1.99	2.10	2.15	1.62
Variance	2.76	3.96	4.42	4.61	2.62
Skewness	0.43	0.96	1.08	0.44	-1.45
Kurtosis	-0.30	-0.25	-0.44	-1.38	1.00
Range	6.00	6.00	6.00	6.00	5.00
Minimum	1.00	1.00	1.00	1.00	2.00
Maximum	7.00	7.00	7.00	7.00	7.00
Sum	129.00	109.00	93.00	113.00	219.00

Note. Based on a scale of 1 (*not implemented*) to 7 (*fully implemented*).
[a] Multiple modes exist. The smallest value is shown.

Participants were asked to define the future utilization of all of the factors: online access to services, online records requests, online permitting, online payments, and online contact information (Table 7). The specific tests for each item included mean, median, mode, standard deviation, variance, range, minimum, maximum, standard error of the mean, skewness, and kurtosis.

Table 7

Descriptive Analysis of E-Government Utilization Variables (Future)

Statistic	Online access to services	Online records requests	Online permitting	Online payments	Online contact information
N					
Valid	34	34	32	34	33
Missing	7	7	9	7	8
Mean	5.03	4.62	4.13	4.68	6.21
Std. error of mean	0.27	0.32	0.34	0.34	0.24
Median	5.00	5.00	4.00	5.00	7.00
Mode	6.00	6.00[a]	2.00[a]	6.00	7.00
Std. deviation	1.55	1.89	1.90	1.97	1.36
Variance	2.39	3.58	3.60	3.86	1.86
Skewness	-0.31	-0.29	0.02	-0.54	-2.14
Kurtosis	-1.02	-1.09	-1.23	-0.88	4.19
Range	5.00	6.00	6.00	6.00	5.00
Minimum	2.00	1.00	1.00	1.00	2.00
Maximum	7.00	7.00	7.00	7.00	7.00
Sum	171.00	157.00	132.00	159.00	205.00

Note. Based on a scale of 1 (*not implemented*) to 7 (*fully implemented*).

[a] Multiple modes exist. The smallest value is shown.

The initial baseline question related to the perceived implementation of e-government (now) provided the foundation for a multiple linear regression model that evaluated the factors contained within the survey question (Table 8). E-government (now) was the dependent variable within the regression model, and online access to services, online records requests, online permitting, online payments, and online contact information represented the independent variables. Using a basic-fit model, the linear regression analysis model summary results indicated R would be .893 with all predictors included. Model results also included R square at .798, adjusted R square at .758, standard error of the estimate .734, and a Durbin-Watson of 1.71. A review of Table 8 illustrated how the various elements of e-government (now) related to the relative dispersion of the baseline variable based on multiple linear regressions. Overall, a significant relationship was seen between online access to services (now), online records requests (now), online permitting (now), and the baseline e-government (now) variable.

Table 8

E-Government (Now) Multiple Linear Regression Coefficients

Variable	Unstandardized coefficients		Standardized coefficients		
	B	*SE*	Beta	*t*	Sig.
(Constant)	1.017	.476		2.136	.043
Online access to services (now)	0.803	.142	.788	5.651	.000
Online records requests (now)	-0.308	.114	-.323	-2.711	.012
Online permitting (now)	0.274	.113	.345	2.424	.023
Online payments (now)	0.058	.092	.080	0.634	.532
Online contact information (now)	-0.093	.090	-.106	-1.034	.311

Note. Dependent variable: E-government (now)

In addition to the baseline question about e-government (now), the survey questionnaire included a baseline question about e-government (future). The baseline question related to the perceived implementation of e-government (future) provided the foundation for a multiple linear regression model that evaluated the factors contained within the survey question. E-government (future) was the dependent variable within the regression model, and online access to services, online records requests, online permitting, online payments, and online contact information represented the independent variables. Using a basic-fit model, the linear regression analysis model summary results indicated R would be .918 with all predictors included. Model results also included R square at .842, adjusted R square at .808, standard error of the estimate .662, and a Durbin-Watson of 2.302. Both online access to services (future) and online records requests (future) had a significant relationship to e-government (future), as shown in Table 9.

Table 9

E-Government (Future) Multiple Linear Regression Coefficients

Variable	Unstandardized coefficients		Standardized coefficients		
	B	*SE*	Beta	*t*	Sig.
(Constant)	1.358	.570		2.383	.026
Online access to services (future)	0.806	.142	.854	5.660	.000
Online records requests (future)	-0.299	.092	-.379	-3.264	.003
Online permitting (future)	0.186	.095	.241	1.967	.061
Online payments (future)	0.125	.091	.163	1.373	.183
Online contact information (future)	-0.062	.109	-.058	-0.570	.574

Note. Dependent variable: E-government (future)

Research Question 2 Results

To what extent do local governments utilize e-feedback? Determination of the extent to which local governments were utilizing e-feedback required the collection of information from participants on their current practices. The survey questionnaire included a matrix style question:

> From your personal experiences and knowledge, rate the current implementation of the following e-feedback collection mechanisms in your city both now and the degree of implementation based on any planned future expansion from 1, being not implemented, to 7, being fully implemented.

Evaluation of the extent to which local governments utilized e-feedback involved asking questions about both current implementation and planned future implementation. In addition to the direct question, the matrix style format allows the participant to evaluate specific elements of e-feedback. Specifically, the participant evaluated the following items: e-feedback, online surveys, online polling, virtual focus groups, e-mail surveys, automated phone surveys, tracking website statistics, and e-government benchmarks. Each of the items measured received statistical testing including descriptive and frequency statistical analysis. The specific tests for each item included mean, median, mode, standard deviation, variance, range, minimum, maximum, standard error of the mean, skewness, and kurtosis.

Table 10 presents descriptive statistical analysis of both e-feedback now and in the future based on mean, median, mode, standard deviation, variance, range, minimum, maximum, standard error of the mean, skewness, and kurtosis. The participants favored the implementation of e-feedback in the future. The range of responses demonstrated that the participants believed e-feedback would be either not implemented or fully implemented.

Table 10

Descriptive Analysis of the E-Feedback Variable (Now and Future)

Statistic	E-feedback now	E-feedback in the future
N		
Valid	37	33
Missing	4	8
Mean	2.92	4.30
Std. error of mean	0.30	0.32
Median	3.00	5.00
Mode	1.00	5.00
Std. deviation	1.83	1.85
Variance	3.35	3.41
Skewness	0.50	-0.41
Kurtosis	-0.76	-0.96
Range	6.00	6.00
Minimum	1.00	1.00
Maximum	7.00	7.00
Sum	108.00	142.00

Note. Based on a scale of 1 (*not implemented*) to 7 (*fully implemented*).

The direct question about e-feedback produced a mean response rate of 2.92, which represented significant room for improvement while indicating that some implementation of e-feedback has occurred. The histogram shown in Figure 5 illustrated that the data were weighted toward the lower end of potential distribution. Comparing the e-feedback (now) to the distribution for e-feedback (future), the data contained within the histogram in Figure 6 represented a more normally distributed response grouping.

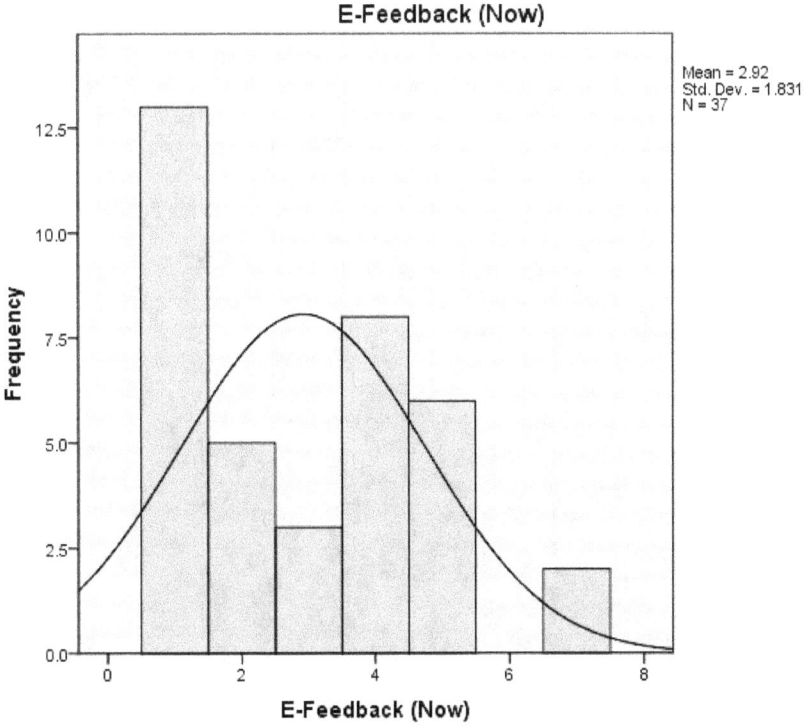

Figure 5. Histogram of e-feedback (now).

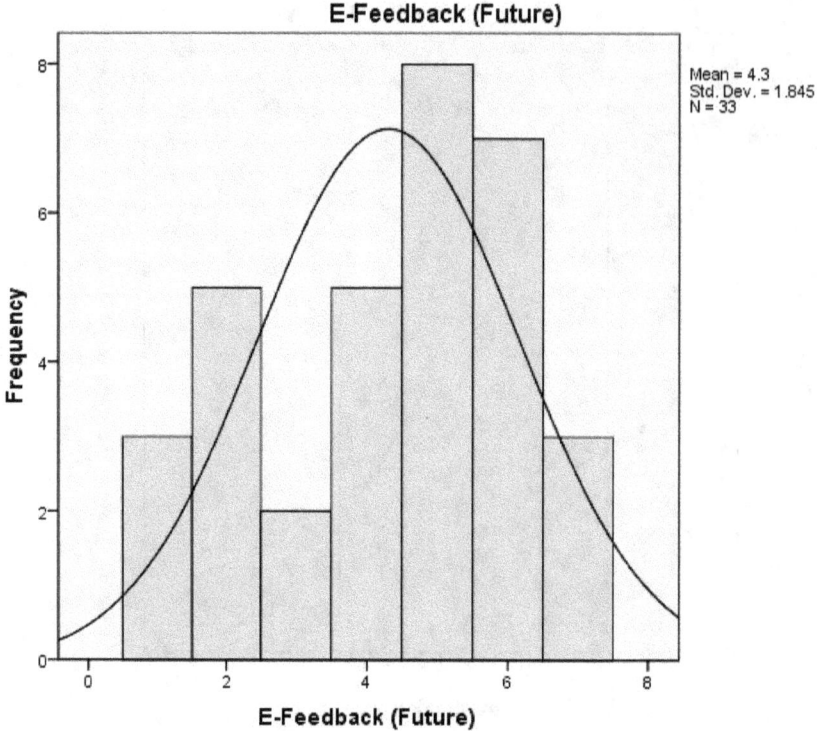

E-Feedback (Future)

Mean = 4.3
Std. Dev. = 1.845
N = 33

Figure 6. Histogram of e-feedback (future).

Table 11 presents the participant evaluations of the current state of the following e-feedback items: online surveys, online polling, virtual focus groups, e-mail surveys, automated phone surveys, tracking website statistics, and e-government benchmarks. Each of the items measured received statistical testing including descriptive and frequency statistical analysis. The specific tests for each item included mean, median, mode, standard deviation, variance, range, minimum, maximum, standard error of the mean, skewness, and kurtosis.

Table 11

Descriptive Analysis of E-Feedback Utilization Variables (Now)

Statistic	Online surveys	Online polling	Virtual focus groups	E-mail surveys	Automated phone surveys	Tracking website statistics	E-gov. benchmarks
N							
Valid	39	37	38	39	37	38	36
Missing	2	4	3	2	4	3	5
Mean	2.46	2.14	1.32	2.33	1.24	3.18	2.08
SE of mean	0.33	0.30	0.13	0.31	0.08	0.37	0.29
Median	1.00	1.00	1.00	1.00	1.00	3.00	1.00
Mode	1.00	1.00	1.00	1.00	1.00	1.00	1.00
SD	2.05	1.84	0.77	1.95	0.49	2.25	1.73
Variance	4.20	3.40	0.60	3.81	0.25	5.07	2.99
Skewness	1.17	1.76	2.68	1.39	1.95	0.46	1.58
Range	6.00	6.00	3.00	6.00	2.00	6.00	6.00
Minimum	1.00	1.00	1.00	1.00	1.00	1.00	1.00
Maximum	7.00	7.00	4.00	7.00	3.00	7.00	7.00
Sum	96.00	79.00	50.00	91.00	46.00	121.00	75.00

Note. Based on a scale of 1 (*not implemented*) to 7 (*fully implemented*).

Table 12 addresses how the participants evaluated the future of the following e-feedback related items: online surveys, online polling, virtual focus groups, e-mail surveys, automated phone surveys, tracking website statistics, and e-government benchmarks. Each of the items measured received statistical testing including descriptive and frequency statistical analysis. The specific tests for each item included mean, median, mode, standard deviation, variance, range, minimum, maximum, standard error of the mean, skewness, and kurtosis.

Table 12

Descriptive Analysis of E-Feedback Utilization Variables (Future)

Statistic	Online surveys	Online polling	Virtual focus groups	E-mail surveys	Automated phone surveys	Tracking website statistics	E-gov. benchmarks
N							
Valid	34	31	31	34	34	33	31
Missing	7	10	10	7	7	8	10
Mean	3.74	2.97	2.06	3.65	1.97	4.24	3.13
SE of mean	0.35	0.35	0.27	0.39	0.28	0.38	0.34
Median	4.00	2.00	1.00	3.50	1.00	4.00	3.00
Mode	2.00	1.00[a]	1.00	1.00	1.00	4.00[a]	1.00
SD	2.05	1.96	1.50	2.25	1.62	2.21	1.88
Variance	4.20	3.83	2.26	5.08	2.64	4.88	3.52
Skewness	0.09	0.70	1.14	0.20	1.95	-0.16	0.35
Range	6.00	6.00	5.00	6.00	6.00	6.00	6.00
Minimum	1.00	1.00	1.00	1.00	1.00	1.00	1.00
Maximum	7.00	7.00	6.00	7.00	7.00	7.00	7.00
Sum	127.00	92.00	64.00	124.00	67.00	140.00	97.00

Note. Based on a scale of 1 (*not implemented*) to 7 (*fully implemented*).
[a] Multiple modes exist. The smallest value is shown.

The initial baseline question related to the perceived implementation of e-feedback (now) provided the foundation for a multiple linear regression model that evaluates the factors contained within the survey question. E-feedback (now) was the dependent variable within the regression model, and the independent variables were online surveys, online polling, virtual focus groups, e-mail surveys, automated phone surveys, tracking website statistics, and e-government benchmarks. Using a basic-fit model, the linear regression analysis model summary results indicated R would be .866 with all predictors included. Model results also included R square at .750, adjusted R square at .683, standard error of the estimate 1.029, and a Durbin-Watson of 2.369. Only online surveys (now) and e-government benchmarks (now) had a significant relationship with the baseline variable of e-feedback (now), as shown in Table 13. With an R of .866, the multiple linear regression model reasonably explained the baseline variable.

Table 13

E-Feedback (Now) Multiple Linear Regression Coefficients

Variable	Unstandardized coefficients		Standardized coefficients		
	B	*SE*	Beta	*t*	Sig.
(Constant)	1.083	.510		2.122	.044
Online surveys (now)	0.531	.242	.570	2.195	.037
Online polling (now)	-0.610	.454	-.560	-1.343	.191
Virtual focus groups (now)	-0.264	.364	-.110	-0.726	.474
E-mail surveys (now)	0.206	.369	.199	0.559	.581
Automated phone surveys (now)	-0.297	.479	-.081	-0.620	.540
Tracking website statistics (now)	0.158	.116	.185	1.364	.184
E-gov. benchmarks (now)	0.723	.154	.698	4.694	.000

Note. Dependent variable: E-feedback (now)

The second baseline question related to the perceived implementation of e-feedback (future) provided the foundation for a multiple linear regression model that evaluated the factors contained within the survey question. E-feedback (future) was the dependent variable within the regression model, and the independent variables were online surveys, online polling, virtual focus groups, e-mail surveys, automated phone surveys, tracking website statistics, and e-government benchmarks. Using a basic-fit model, the linear regression analysis model summary results indicated R would be .871 with all predictors included. Model results also included R square at .759, adjusted R square at .675, standard error of the estimate 1.062, and a Durbin-Watson of 2.023. A very strong relationship existed between e-feedback (future) and e-government benchmarks (future), as shown in Table 14.

Table 14

E-Feedback (Future) Multiple Linear Regression Coefficients

Variable	Unstandardized coefficients		Standardized coefficients	*t*	Sig.
	B	*SE*	Beta		
(Constant)	1.438	.497		2.893	.009
Online surveys (future)	0.419	.256	.463	1.639	.117
Online polling (future)	0.021	.210	.021	0.101	.921
Virtual focus groups (now)	-0.124	.237	-.101	-0.522	.607
E-mail surveys (future)	-0.213	.230	-.247	-0.927	.365
Automated phone surveys (future)	0.070	.209	.065	0.337	.740
Tracking website statistics (future)	-0.125	.126	-.151	-0.999	.330
E-gov. benchmarks (future)	0.765	.209	.803	3.660	.002

Note. Dependent variable: E-feedback (future)

Research Question 3 Results

To what extent do local governments audit the information collected from e-feedback implementations? The third research question investigated to what extent local governments audited the information collected from e-feedback implementations. To test this conjecture, a matrix style question from the mail survey stated,

> The following question attempts to evaluate what local governments are doing to audit the information collected from e-feedback implementations. From your personal experiences and knowledge within local government, rate the auditing of e-feedback data (e.g., from online surveys, online polling, virtual focus groups, or e-mail surveys) in your city both now and the degree of implementation based on any planned future expansion from 1, being not implemented, to 7, being fully implemented.

Specifically, the matrix style question included the following items: auditing e-feedback, general auditing functions, auditing decision making, auditing strategic planning, budget auditing, auditing workforce, auditing automation, independent auditing, internal staff evaluation, optimization modeling, improving e-government, expanding e-government, and developing public policy. Each of the items measured received statistical testing, including descriptive and frequency statistical analysis. The specific tests for each item included mean, median, mode, standard deviation, variance, range, minimum, maximum, standard error of the mean, skewness, and kurtosis (Table 15).

Table 15

Descriptive Analysis of the Auditing E-Feedback (Now and Future)

Statistic	Auditing e-feedback now	Auditing e-feedback in the future
N		
Valid	33	28
Missing	8	13
Mean	2.21	3.11
Std. error of mean	0.30	0.35
Median	1.00	3.00
Mode	1.00	2.00
Std. deviation	1.71	1.83
Variance	2.92	3.36
Skewness	1.33	0.69
Kurtosis	0.39	-0.45
Range	5.00	6.00
Minimum	1.00	1.00
Maximum	6.00	7.00
Sum	73.00	87.00

Note. Based on a scale of 1 (*not implemented*) to 7 (*fully implemented*).

A comparison of basic descriptive statistics illustrated the differences between auditing e-feedback now and in the future. The mean response to auditing e-feedback (now), at 2.21, was lower than the 3.11 mean of auditing e-feedback (future). A difference in range existed between the two variables, with auditing e-feedback (future) having a maximum value of 7 instead of the 6 that auditing e-feedback (now) received, representing a difference in expected future implementation.

The responses included in the auditing e-feedback (now) histogram illustrated a large divergence in implementation (Figure 7). With a mean response of 2.21, the participants perceived that auditing e-feedback was barely implemented within local governments.

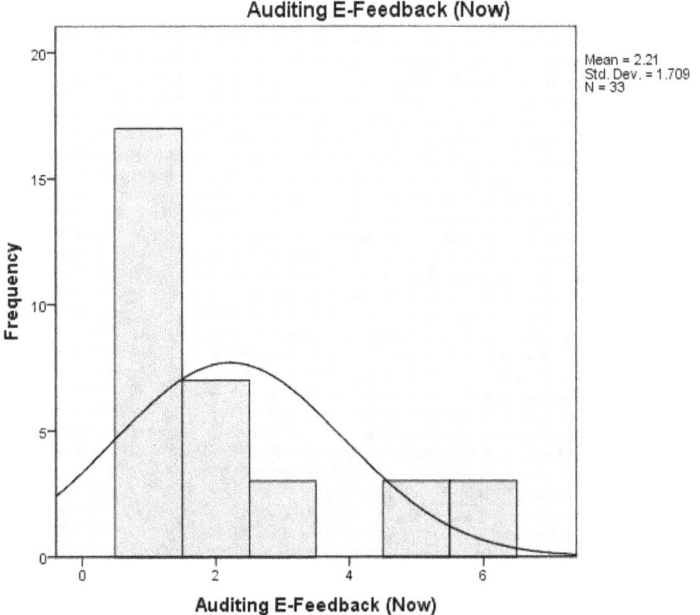

Figure 7. Histogram of auditing e-feedback (now).
Overall the dispersion of auditing e-feedback (future) painted a very limited picture of future implementation (Figure 8). With a mean response of 3.11, the direct question auditing e-feedback (future) variable had the lowest future planned implementation of any of the other future-related direct questions.

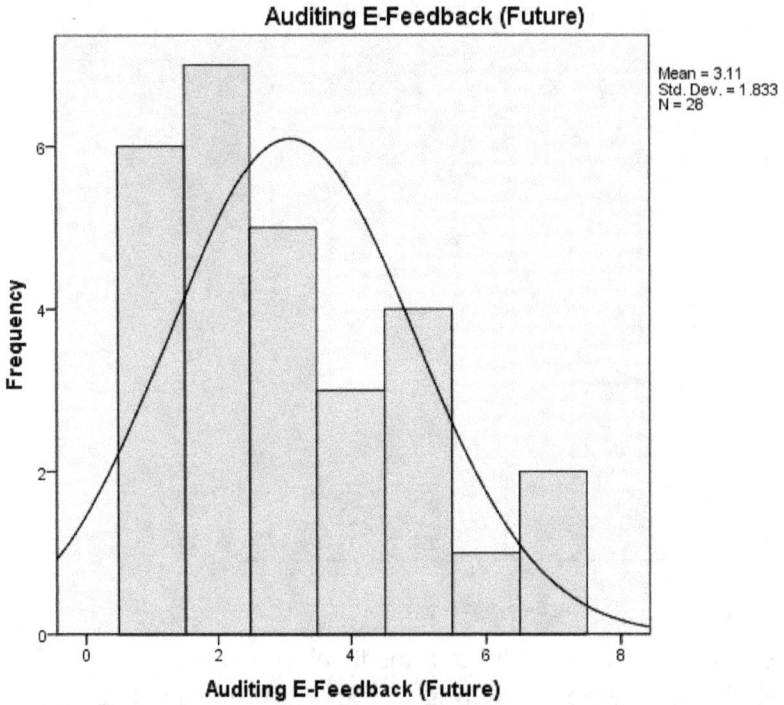

Figure 8. Histogram of auditing e-feedback (future).

Table 16 illustrates how the participants evaluated several elements related to the current state of auditing e-feedback: general auditing functions, auditing decision making, auditing strategic planning, budget auditing, auditing workforce, and auditing automation. The specific tests for each item included mean, median, mode, standard deviation, variance, range, minimum, maximum, standard error of the mean, skewness, and kurtosis.

Table 16

Descriptive Analysis of Auditing E-Feedback Variables 1–7 (Now)

Statistic	General auditing functions	Auditing citizen interaction	Auditing decision making	Auditing strategic planning	Budget auditing	Auditing workforce	Auditing automation
N							
Valid	34	35	34	34	33	34	34
Missing	7	6	7	7	8	7	7
Mean	2.38	2.03	1.76	1.71	1.97	1.79	1.71
SE of mean	0.33	0.27	0.24	0.20	0.29	0.25	0.20
Median	1.00	1.00	1.00	1.00	1.00	1.00	1.00
Mode	1.00	1.00	1.00	1.00	1.00	1.00	1.00
SD	1.91	1.62	1.39	1.14	1.65	1.43	1.19
Variance	3.64	2.62	1.94	1.31	2.72	2.05	1.43
Skewness	1.28	1.68	2.16	2.05	1.70	1.90	1.97
Kurtosis	0.51	2.14	4.10	4.97	2.12	2.87	4.07
Range	6.00	6.00	5.00	5.00	6.00	5.00	5.00
Minimum	1.00	1.00	1.00	1.00	1.00	1.00	1.00
Maximum	7.00	7.00	6.00	6.00	7.00	6.00	6.00
Sum	81.00	71.00	60.00	58.00	65.00	61.00	58.00

Note. Based on a scale of 1 (*not implemented*) to 7 (*fully implemented*).

The first seven auditing e-feedback variables (now) are presented in Table 16; the remaining six are presented in Table 17. Table 17 illustrates how the participants evaluated independent auditing, internal staff evaluation, optimization modeling, improving e-government, expanding e-government, and developing public policy.

Table 17

Descriptive Analysis of Auditing E-Feedback Variables 8–14 (Now)

Statistic	Independent auditing	Internal staff evaluation	Optimization modeling	Numerical modeling	Improving e-gov.	Expanding e-gov.	Developing public policy
N							
Valid	33	34	33	32	34	34	34
Missing	8	7	8	9	7	7	7
Mean	1.88	2.20	1.48	1.25	2.59	2.76	2.15
SE of mean	0.27	0.30	0.20	0.10	0.31	0.36	0.25
Median	1.00	1.00	1.00	1.00	2.00	2.00	1.00
Mode	1.00	1.00	1.00	1.00	1.00	1.00	1.00
SD	1.54	1.77	1.18	0.57	1.81	2.08	1.48
Variance	2.36	3.14	1.38	0.32	3.28	4.31	2.19
Skewness	1.87	1.41	2.86	2.25	0.79	0.79	1.04
Kurtosis	3.03	0.87	8.15	4.26	-0.44	-0.80	-0.01
Range	6.00	6.00	5.00	2.00	6.00	6.00	5.00
Minimum	1.00	1.00	1.00	1.00	1.00	1.00	1.00
Maximum	7.00	7.00	6.00	3.00	7.00	7.00	6.00
Sum	62.00	75.00	49.00	40.00	88.00	94.00	73.00

Note. Based on a scale of 1 (*not implemented*) to 7 (*fully implemented*).

Table 18 illustrates how the participant evaluated several elements related to the future state of auditing e-feedback including: general auditing functions, auditing decision making, auditing strategic planning, budget auditing, auditing workforce, and auditing automation. The specific tests for each item included mean, median, mode, standard deviation, variance, range, minimum, maximum, standard error of the mean, skewness, and kurtosis.

Table 18

Descriptive Analysis of Auditing E-Feedback Variables 1–7 (Future)

Statistic	General auditing functions	Auditing citizen interaction	Auditing decision making	Auditing strategic planning	Budget auditing	Auditing workforce	Auditing automation
N							
Valid	28	29	27	28	27	28	28
Missing	13	12	14	13	14	13	13
Mean	2.79	2.76	2.41	2.64	2.89	2.29	2.18
SE of mean	0.37	0.34	0.33	0.33	0.37	0.34	0.31
Median	2.00	2.00	2.00	2.00	2.00	1.50	2.00
Mode	1.00	1.00	1.00	1.00	1.00	1.00	1.00
SD	1.95	1.83	1.72	1.75	1.91	1.80	1.66
Variance	3.80	3.33	2.94	3.05	3.64	3.25	2.75
Skewness	1.00	0.80	1.28	1.00	0.85	1.42	1.70
Kurtosis	-0.20	-0.46	0.86	0.02	-0.33	0.95	2.21
Range	6.00	6.00	6.00	6.00	6.00	6.00	6.00
Minimum	1.00	1.00	1.00	1.00	1.00	1.00	1.00
Maximum	7.00	7.00	7.00	7.00	7.00	7.00	7.00
Sum	78.00	80.00	65.00	74.00	78.00	64.00	61.00

Note. Based on a scale of 1 (*not implemented*) to 7 (*fully implemented*)

Table 19 illustrates how the participants evaluated the remaining elements related to the current state of auditing e-feedback: independent auditing, internal staff evaluation, optimization modeling, improving e-government, expanding e-government, and developing public policy. The specific tests for each item included mean, median, mode, standard deviation, variance, range, minimum, maximum, standard error of the mean, skewness, and kurtosis.

Table 19

Descriptive Analysis of Auditing E-Feedback Variables 8–14 (Future)

Statistic	Independent auditing	Internal staff evaluation	Optimization modeling	Numerical modeling	Improving e-gov.	Expanding e-gov.	Developing public policy
N							
Valid	26	28	28	28	30	30	28
Missing	15	13	13	13	11	11	13
Mean	2.27	2.61	2.07	1.82	3.73	3.70	3.18
SE of mean	0.37	0.38	0.35	0.28	0.41	0.42	0.36
Median	1.00	2.00	1.00	1.00	3.50	3.50	3.00
Mode	1.00	1.00	1.00	1.00	1.00	1.00	1.00
SD	1.87	2.01	1.86	1.49	2.23	2.28	1.89
Variance	3.49	4.03	3.48	2.23	4.96	5.18	3.56
Skewness	1.41	1.12	1.88	2.06	0.20	0.21	0.33
Kurtosis	0.79	-0.05	2.44	3.39	-1.43	-1.54	-1.43
Range	6.00	6.00	6.00	5.00	6.00	6.00	5.00
Minimum	1.00	1.00	1.00	1.00	1.00	1.00	1.00
Maximum	7.00	7.00	7.00	6.00	7.00	7.00	6.00
Sum	59.00	73.00	58.00	51.00	112.00	111.00	89.00

Note. Based on a scale of 1 (*not implemented*) to 7 (*fully implemented*).

The initial baseline question related to the perceived implementation of auditing e-feedback (now) provided the foundation for a multiple linear regression model that evaluated the factors contained within the survey question. Auditing e-feedback (now) was the dependent variable within the regression model, and the independent variables were auditing e-feedback, general auditing functions, auditing decision making, auditing strategic planning, budget auditing, auditing workforce, auditing automation, independent auditing, internal staff evaluation, optimization modeling, improving e-government, expanding e-government, and developing public policy (Table 20). Using a basic-fit model, the linear regression analysis model summary results indicated R would be .999 with all predictors included. Model results also included R square at .997, adjusted R square at .995, standard error of the estimate 0.112, and a Durbin-Watson of 2.302.

Table 20

Auditing E-Feedback (Now) Multiple Linear Regression Coefficients

Variable	Unstandardized coefficients		Standardized coefficients		
	B	*SE*	Beta	*t*	Sig.
(Constant)	-0.015	.125		-0.119	.907
General auditing functions (now)	0.615	.051	0.735	11.962	.000
Auditing citizen interaction (now)	-0.137	.054	-0.127	-2.515	.025
Auditing decision making (now)	-0.933	.082	-0.730	-11.412	.000
Auditing strategic planning (now)	1.784	.161	0.935	11.098	.000
Budget auditing (now)	-1.523	.102	-1.668	-14.942	.000
Auditing workforce (now)	0.997	.072	0.763	13.815	.000
Auditing automation (now)	-1.212	.049	-0.727	-24.763	.000
Independent auditing (now)	0.166	.047	0.153	3.517	.003
Internal staff evaluation (now)	0.318	.052	0.318	6.076	.000
Optimization modeling (now)	1.713	.179	0.920	9.588	.000
Numerical modeling (now)	-1.192	.256	-0.370	-4.665	.000
Improving e-government (now)	0.044	.076	0.047	0.586	.568
Expanding e-government (now)	0.651	.094	0.841	6.955	.000

Note. Dependent variable: Auditing e-feedback (now)

The second baseline question related to the perceived implementation of auditing e-feedback (future) provided the foundation for a multiple linear regression model that evaluated the factors contained within the survey question. Auditing e-feedback (future) was the dependent variable within the regression model, and the independent variables were auditing e-feedback, general auditing functions, auditing decision making, auditing strategic planning, budget auditing, auditing workforce, auditing automation, independent auditing, internal staff evaluation, optimization modeling, improving e-government, expanding e-government, and developing public policy (Table 21). Using a basic-fit model, the linear regression analysis model summary results indicated R would be .938 with all predictors included. Model results also included R square at .879, adjusted R square at .691, standard error of the estimate 0.969, and a Durbin-Watson of 1.863.

Table 21

Auditing E-Feedback (Future) Multiple Linear Regression Coefficients

Variable	Unstandardized coefficients		Standardized coefficients	*t*	Sig.
	B	*SE*	Beta		
(Constant)	0.316	0.496		0.637	.540
General auditing functions (future)	-0.632	0.676	-0.675	-0.934	.375
Auditing citizen interaction (future)	1.099	0.641	1.068	1.714	.121
Auditing decision making (future)	0.969	1.218	0.852	0.796	.447
Auditing strategic planning (future)	-0.043	0.757	-0.040	-0.057	.955
Budget auditing (future)	0.069	0.383	0.078	0.180	.861
Auditing workforce (future)	3.107	2.218	2.855	1.401	.195
Auditing automation (future)	-6.943	3.950	-5.756	-1.758	.113
Independent auditing (future)	0.663	1.038	0.721	0.639	.539
Internal staff evaluation (future)	0.354	0.447	0.378	0.794	.448
Optimization modeling (future)	-6.017	3.582	-5.820	-1.680	.127
Numerical modeling (future)	8.084	4.441	7.237	1.821	.102
Improving e-government (future)	0.554	0.555	0.707	0.998	.344
Expanding e-government (future)	0.081	0.581	0.105	0.139	.892

Note. Dependent variable: Auditing e-feedback (future)

Research Question 4 Results

Does a statistically positive relationship exist between the implementation of local e-government services and e-feedback collection methods that increase governmental responsiveness through citizen participation? The fourth research question involved a testable conjecture. Two bivariate correlation tests were performed for this research question. First, a bivariate correlation test was conducted of the degree of implementation of e-government services as a composite variable and the degree of implementation of e-feedback collection methods as a composite variable (Table 22). Second, a bivariate correlation testing of the degree of implementation of e-government services and the degree of implementation of e-feedback collection methods was conducted.

Table 22

E-Government Correlation to E-Feedback

Statistic	E-government (now)	E-feedback (now)	E-government (future)	E-feedback (future)
E-government (now)				
Pearson correlation	1	.626**	.648**	.424*
Sig. (2-tailed)		.000	.000	.016
Sum of squares & cross products	92.306	66.083	40.576	34.031
Covariance	2.637	1.888	1.268	1.098
N	36	36	33	32
E-feedback (now)				
Pearson correlation	.626**	1	.496**	.796**
Sig. (2-tailed)	.000		.003	.000
Sum of squares & cross products	66.083	120.757	36.545	74.121
Covariance	1.888	3.354	1.142	2.316
N	36	37	33	33
E-government (future)				
Pearson correlation	.648**	.496**	1	.539**
Sig. (2-tailed)	.000	.003		.001
Sum of squares & cross products	40.576	36.545	65.879	45.156
Covariance	1.268	1.142	2.059	1.457
N	33	33	33	32
E-feedback (future)				
Pearson correlation	.424*	.796**	.539**	1
Sig. (2-tailed)	.016	.000	.001	
Sum of squares & cross products	34.031	74.121	45.156	108.970
Covariance	1.098	2.316	1.457	3.405
N	32	33	32	33

$*p \le .05$ (2-tailed). $**p \le .01$ (2-tailed).

Research Question 5 Results

Does a statistically positive relationship exist between the implementation of local e-feedback mechanisms and auditing functions utilizing the information collected from e-feedback mechanisms? The fifth research question involved a testable conjecture. Two bivariate correlation tests were performed for this research question. First, a bivariate correlation testing was conducted of the degree of implementation of e-feedback services as a composite variable and the degree of implementation of auditing e-feedback collection methods as a composite variable. Second, a bivariate correlation testing of the degree of implementation of e-feedback services and the degree of implementation of auditing using e-feedback methods was conducted (Table 23).

Table 23

E-Feedback Correlation to Auditing E-Feedback

Statistic	E-feedback (now)	Auditing e-feedback (now)	E-feedback (future)	Auditing e-feedback (future)
E-feedback (now)				
Pearson correlation	1	.552**	.796**	.445*
Sig. (2-tailed)		.001	.000	.018
Sum of squares & cross products	120.757	56.848	74.121	33.964
Covariance	3.354	1.777	2.316	1.258
N	37	33	33	28
Auditing e-feedback (now)				
Pearson correlation	.552**	1	.646**	.775**
Sig. (2-tailed)	.001		.000	.000
Sum of squares & cross products	56.848	93.515	54.552	56.704
Covariance	1.777	2.922	1.948	2.181
N	33	33	29	27
E-feedback (future)				
Pearson correlation	.796**	.646**	1	.635**
Sig. (2-tailed)	.000	.000		.000
Sum of squares & cross products	74.121	54.552	108.970	56.571
Covariance	2.316	1.948	3.405	2.095
N	33	29	33	28
Auditing e-feedback (future)				
Pearson correlation	.445*	.775**	.635**	1
Sig. (2-tailed)	.018	.000	.000	
Sum of squares & cross products	33.964	56.704	56.571	90.679
Covariance	1.258	2.181	2.095	3.358
N	28	27	28	28

*$p <= .05$ (2-tailed). **$p <= .01$ (2-tailed).

Survey Data From the Census of Government

Each of the randomly selected local governments had certain information available within the Census of Government. For example, the survey instrument did not need to collect information

91

about the form of government, total population, budget, or population demographics. This descriptive statistical information was publicly available and did not require collection through the deployment of a survey instrument.

Local Government Grouping Protocol

With the survey universe, a grouping protocol involved categorizing each of the randomly selected local governments by population. A separation of the metropolitan statistical areas and micropolitan statistical areas enhanced the relevance of the statistical analysis conducted utilizing the survey results. Out of the 41 responses to the survey questionnaire, certain elements of the local government received some descriptive statistical analysis. Total population, total housing units, the population involved in the labor force, and the median household income received tests, including mean, median, mode, standard deviation, variance, range, minimum, maximum, standard error of the mean, skewness, and kurtosis (Table 24). Overall, the population of the local governments included in the survey ranged between 1,440 and 894,943. The mean population of 55,789 indicated a relatively low population for the average responding local government. Based on the sample data the results apply to the represented demographic.

Table 24

Local Government Descriptive Statistics

Statistic	Total population	Housing units	Population in labor force	Median household income
Mean	55,789.37	21,333.90	29,211.59	36,139.71
SE of mean	21,860.76	7,027.16	11,247.94	1,633.63
Median	23,003.00	9,151.00	10,010.00	34,051.00
Mode	8,820.00[a]	4,311.00[a]	4,522.00[a]	26,851.00[a]
SD	139,977.13	44,995.769	72,021.956	10,460.33
Variance	1.959E10	2.025E9	5.187E9	1.094E8
Skewness	5.69	5.20	5.55	1.57
Kurtosis	34.35	29.63	32,924.00	3.33
Range	893,503.00	281,341.00	455,802.00	49,717.00
Minimum	1,440.00	500.00	839.00	20,526.00
Maximum	894,943.00	281,841.00	456,641.00	70,243.00
Sum	2,287,364.00	874,690.00	1,197,675.00	1,481,728.00

Note. $N = 41$.

[a]Multiple modes exist. The smallest value is shown.

Comparing the scatter plot dispersion of the total population, total housing units, the population involved in the labor force, and the median household income showed outliers (Figure 9). Overall, the majority of local governments included in the survey were smaller. The mean participant population of 55,789 also indicated that smaller local governments had a higher response rate.

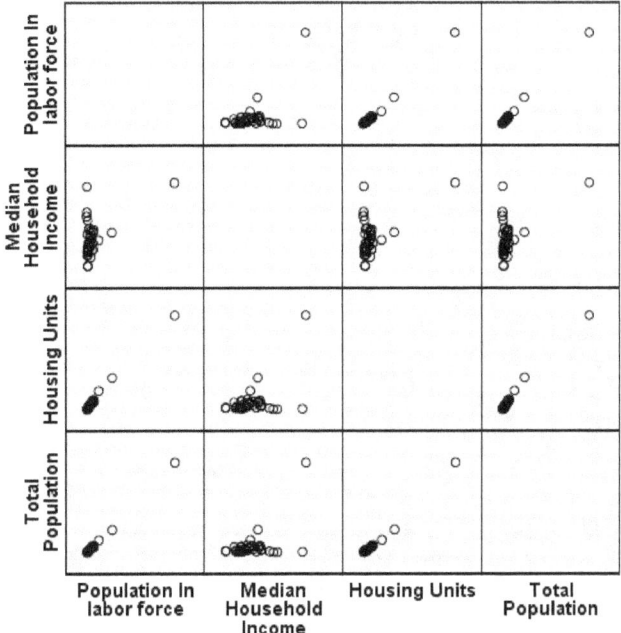

Figure 9. Local government data four-variable comparison scatter plot.

The total population variable of local governments that responded to the survey illustrates the vast majority had total populations lower than 40,000 people. Figure 10 shows that the standard deviation of 139,977 people is associated with the bimodal distribution.

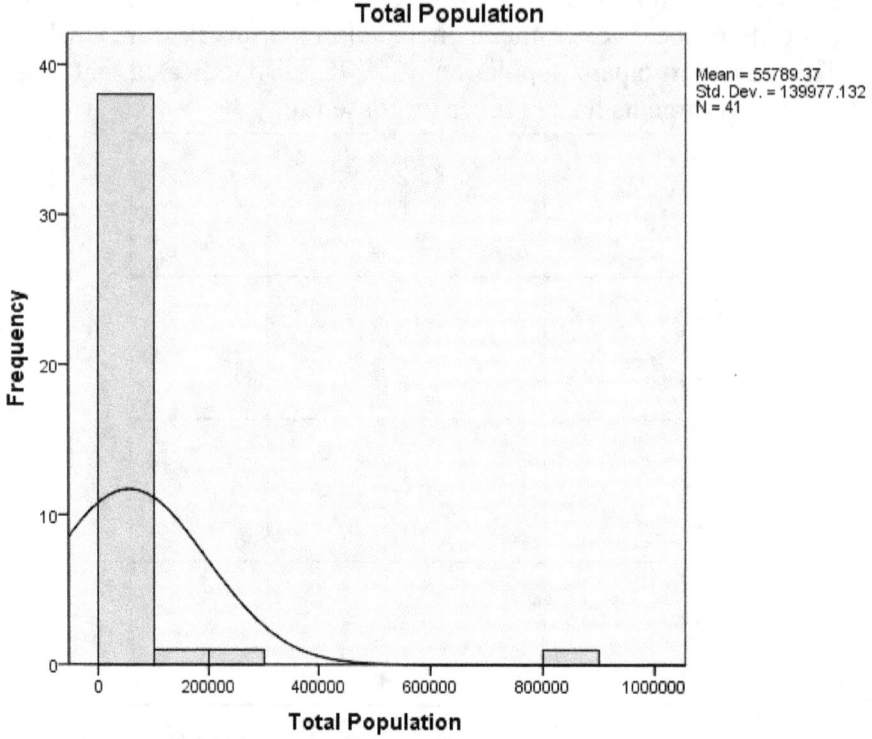

Figure 10. Histogram of total population.

The histogram of total housing units illustrates a similar bimodal distribution to the total population histogram (Figure 11). Housing units provided a secondary indicator of local government size. In conjunction with total population, the two variables provided a reasonable overview the size of the local governments included in the study.

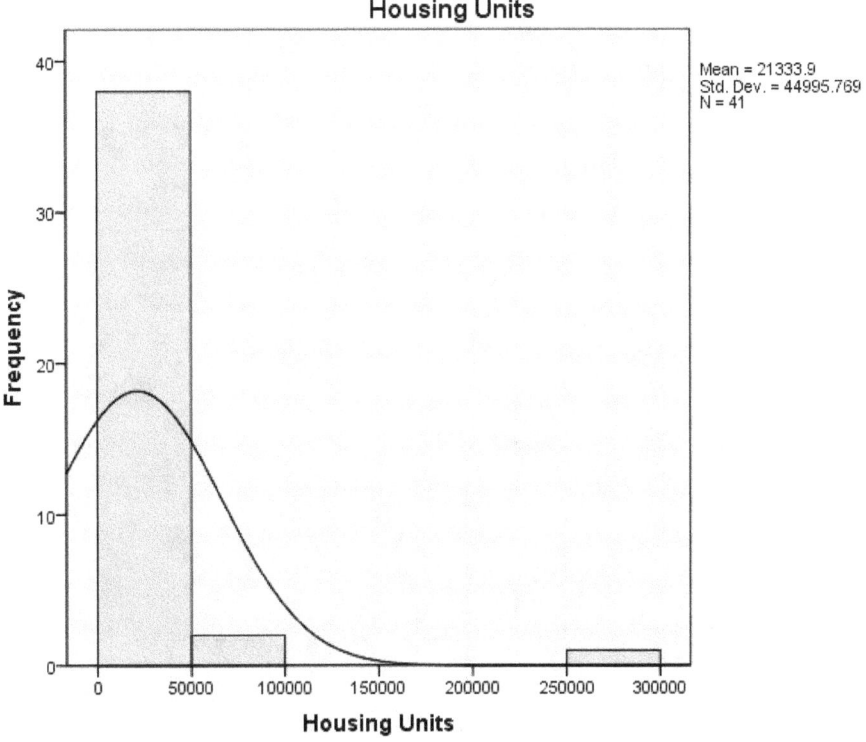

Figure 11. Histogram of total housing units.
The distribution of the median household income of the sample
provided evidence of stronger clustering than the total population
variable. With a standard deviation of 10,640.33, the median
household income had a range between $20,526 and $70,243 (Figure
12).

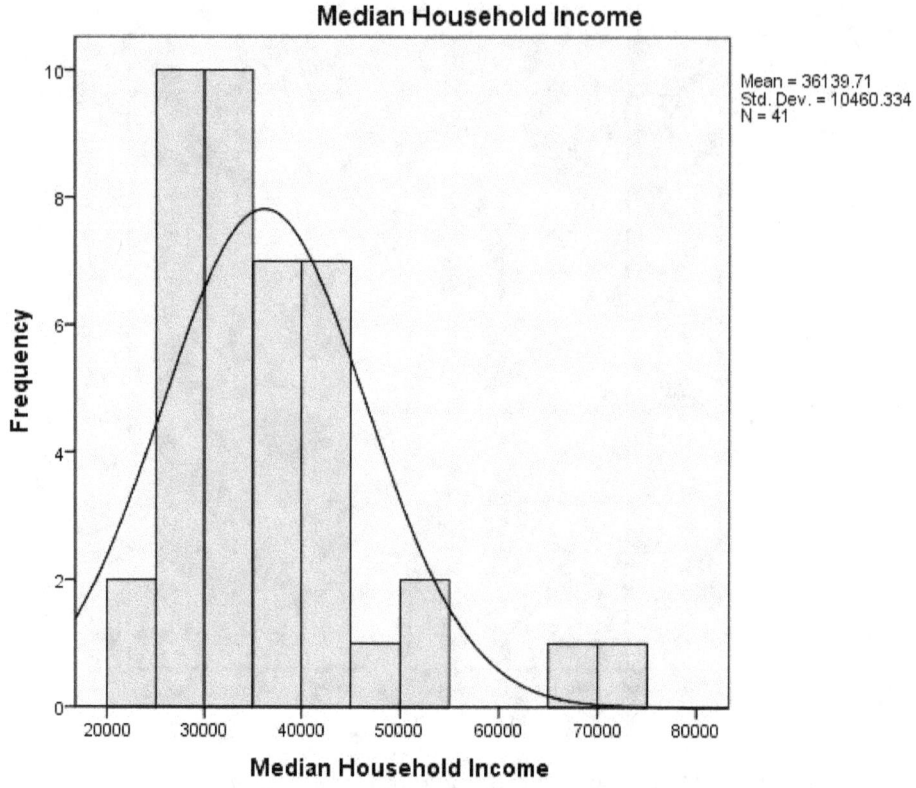

Figure 12. Histogram of median household income.

Chapter Summary

Contained within Chapter 4 were statistics and results that together represented my endeavor to communicate the findings of the survey. The results chapter stated procedural survey notes are provided to ensure full disclosure of all relevant aspects of the research methodology implementation. Reporting was provided to explain how ethical protections were used during the study to protect the participants. Following the procedural notes, a section defined the survey response rate followed by a section that explained the steps taken to adhere to the findings presentation guidelines defined in Chapter 3. Finally, Chapter 4 reported the findings for the five research questions, including numerous tables and graphs. Chapter 5 provides conclusions of the study.

Chapter 5: Conclusions
Study Overview
This study addressed an overarching area of research: the process of implementing e-feedback mechanisms and developing auditing functions using e-feedback. To address the formation of a bureaucratic structure around e-feedback, the study was designed to determine to what extent the presence of e-feedback mechanisms within local e-government implementations indicates the development of bureaucracy based on such e-feedback. The research was guided by five research questions:

1. To what extent do local governments utilize e-government?
2. To what extent do local governments utilize e-feedback?
3. To what extent do local governments audit the information collected from e-feedback implementations?
4. Does a statistically significant, positive relationship exist between the implementation of local e-government services and e-feedback collection methods that increase governmental responsiveness through citizen participation?
5. Does a statistically significant, positive relationship exist between the implementation of local e-feedback mechanisms and auditing functions utilizing the information collected from e-feedback mechanisms?

Research Methods
The sampling universe defined for the study limited the number of potential participants. In this case, the sampling universe or the total number of potential participants was finite. The Office of Management and Budget (2008) provided a list of 953 metropolitan and micropolitan statistical areas in the United States. Using these statistical areas provided a defined sampling universe that represented the largest potential interaction between citizens and government online. A methodology had to be established to communicate with the participants within the sampling universe.

In order to query participants found within the sampling universe, this study used a quantitative, descriptive field survey to collect information from a defined population (McNabb, 2002). The survey participants were selected using simple random sampling. All potential participants had an equal chance of participation in the probability-based study (McNabb, 2002). A sample size was determined based on Cochran's (1977) sample-size formula for continuous data and Cochran's correction formula in conjunction with Salkind's (1997) suggested oversampling by 40% or 50%. The resulting simple random sample included 158 metropolitan and micropolitan statistical areas in the United States. The oversampling recommended by Salkind resulted in the sample size representing 16% of the total sampling universe.

A field survey involving a self-administered questionnaire was sent to the participants to define the current state of a phenomenon like e-feedback collection methods and e-government services (McNabb, 2002). Sixteen pretest surveys and 158 surveys were sent via the U.S. Postal Service; a total of three letters were returned without postage (the stamps must have fallen off during the handling process), and three were returned with an invalid address error. Addresses were identified using the Census of Government database. All survey questionnaires returned to the post office box were included in the study. I coded each survey and entered data into the SPSS software. Each survey was entered in sections and checked against the original survey questionnaire. All questionnaires were entered using the same method. Any outliers were checked against the source material to ensure that the coding process occurred without any errors.

Interpretation of Findings

Findings for Research Question 1

To what extent did local governments utilize e-government? Most local governments are utilizing e-government in limited and specialized ways. Participants who completed the questionnaire perceived e-government (now) as being 48% implemented and future implementation of e-government to hit 72%. Overall, e-government implementation within local governments appeared to be occurring and should be expanding in the near term. Out of the 36 responses to the survey question about the current state of e-government, a mean response of 3.36 out of 7 was established. (The survey questionnaire used a 7-point semantic differential scale.) In response to the same question about the implementation of e-government in the future, 33 survey responses established a mean response of 5.06, establishing expectations for e-government expansion (Table 5). A deeper understanding of the utilization of e-government can be derived from evaluating several specific factors indicative of e-government usage. Specifically the following indicators formed a composite variable that helped assess to what extent local governments utilize e-government: online access to services, online records requests, online permitting, online payments, and online contact information. Together the composite variable for e-government utilization yielded a mean response of 3.50, with a mean response of 4.93 for future e-government utilization, establishing an expected increase of 1.42 based on current expectations for the composite variables (Table 6).

Table 6 provides an overview of the different elements of e-government (now) evaluated within the survey questionnaire. The online contact information (now) variable provided the largest degree of current implementation. Within the spectrum of potential e-government implementations, the online billboard approach of presenting contact information online probably has the fewest potential barriers to implementation. More difficult tasks like online records requests and online permitting have a lower degree of implementation than the comparatively simpler task of allowing online payments.

The e-government (future) question allowed participants to speculate about the degree of future implementation. Overall, the online-contact variable had the highest future implementation with a mean response of 6.21 (Table 7). All of the elements of e-government (future) showed an expected increase in deployment by local governments. The regression models presented in Tables 8 and 9 explain the relationship between the baseline e-government questions and the corresponding elements that received attention within the survey questionnaire. E-government (now) had an overall R of .893, whereas e-government future had a potential R of .918. The increase in R for the e-government (future) multiple regression model indicated a potential overall increase in future deployment.

Findings for Research Question 2

To what extent did local governments utilize e-feedback? Moving one step beyond e-government, the second research question evaluated e-feedback using the same methodology. Compared to the utilization of e-government, fewer local governments are utilizing e-feedback. About 42% of local governments are currently using e-feedback, with an expected increase to 61% in the future. The response count for both e-feedback variables (now and in the future) was different than the response count for the e-government question. Out of the 37 responses to the question about the current state of e-feedback, a mean response of 2.92 was established. With only 33 responses, the question about the future implementation of e-feedback yielded a mean response of 4.30, establishing an expected increase for e-feedback. Instead of solely relaying on the direct question to evaluate the utilization of e-feedback by local governments, a composite variable was built including online surveys, online polling, virtual focus groups, e-mail surveys, automated phone surveys, tracking website statistics, and e-government benchmarks. Combined the composite variable for e-feedback yielded a mean response of 2.11 for current utilization and a mean response of 3.11 for future utilization, establishing an expected increase in e-feedback utilization in the future. Overall, the participants perceived current and future expected utilization of e-feedback as lower than that of e-government.

As shown in Table 11, only one of the e-feedback elements showed a mean response greater than 3: tracking website statistics. The overall trend between e-feedback now and in the future showed that the participants favored implementation to some degree. E-feedback (now) showed a regression model R of .750, compared to the R of e-feedback (future) at .759. Both now and in the future, e-government benchmarks and online surveys provide the best indicators of e-feedback deployment.

Findings for Research Question 3

To what extent did local governments audit the information collected from e-feedback implementations? In the future, only 44% of local governments intend to audit the information collected from e-feedback implementations. Compared to e-government and e-feedback, the participants only considered auditing e-feedback as 32% currently implemented within local governments. The outlook for auditing e-feedback remains relatively limited, with an expected total potential implementation of 44% in the future. Just as the average mean of e-feedback was lower than the average mean of e-government utilization within local government, a decrease in information auditing from e-feedback methods was observed. Out of 33 responses, the direct question about auditing e-feedback resulted in a mean response of 2.21 for current usage. With only 28 responses, the future expectation for auditing using e-feedback methods had a smaller number of total responses than any other category. The mean response for future auditing using e-feedback was 3.11. Instead of purely relying on a direct question about auditing e-feedback, a composite variable of several different elements was utilized.

Specifically, the independent elements forming the composite variable were general auditing functions, auditing citizen interaction, auditing decision making, auditing strategic planning, budget auditing, auditing workforce, auditing automation, independent auditing, internal staff evaluation, optimization modeling, numerical modeling, improving e-government, expanding e-government, and developing public policy. As a composite variable the independent factors reflective of auditing using e-feedback produced a mean response of 1.98 and future auditing using e-feedback produced a mean response of 2.67. A smaller response rate and mean response for auditing using e-feedback data compared to local government utilization of e-government or strictly collecting e-feedback was expected, due to the limited nature of current implementation and utilization.

Findings for Research Question 4

Did a statistically positive relationship exist between the implementation of local e-government services and e-feedback collection methods that increase governmental responsiveness through citizen participation? Within local governments, the concepts of e-government services and e-feedback collection methods are related. A statistically positive relationship existed between local government implementation and utilization of e-government and e-feedback. Using a Pearson correlation (Pearson product-moment correlation coefficient) test at the .05 level (2-tailed), a significant correlation was found between e-government and e-feedback both now and in the future (Table 22). However, the Pearson correlation test at the .01 level (2-tailed) indicated no statistically positive relationship between e-government (now) and e-feedback in the future (Table 22).

Findings for Research Question 5

Did a statistically positive relationship exist between the implementation of local e-feedback mechanisms and auditing functions utilizing the information collected from e-feedback mechanisms? The implementation of local e-feedback mechanisms and auditing functions utilizing the information collected from e-feedback mechanisms within local governments are related. A statistically positive relationship existed between local government implementation and utilization of e-feedback and auditing using e-feedback. Using a Pearson correlation test at the .05 level (2-tailed), a significant correlation was found between e-feedback and auditing using e-feedback both now and in the future (Table 23). However, the Pearson correlation test was not statistically significant at the .01 level (2-tailed).

Implications for Social Change

Academic thinkers such as Putnam (2000) have argued increasing citizen participation in government is a significant and meaningful challenge. Positive social change with respect to citizen participation in government would make a meaningful contribution to strengthening the social fabric within the United States. Consider that several respected scholars (Barber, 1984; Macedo, 2005; Skocpol, 2003) have argued that a decline in citizen participation within democratic processes could risk the very foundations of democracy. This study contributes positively to the literature related to citizen participation in government by expanding understanding of how current e-government implementations utilize e-feedback methods. Proactively increasing understanding of how to improve online service delivery will contribute to positive social change by actively facilitating citizen participation in government.

Professional Application

E-government, e-feedback, and auditing e-feedback are active topics in public administration. Practitioners within the field of public administration need mechanisms and best-practice examples for utilizing e-feedback to increase citizen satisfaction (Norris & Lloyd, 2006). Identification of otherwise unrelated or uncoordinated elements can help practitioners benefit from the advancement of theory development and theory testing (McNabb, 2002).

Contribution to Social Change

Increased governmental responsiveness directly benefits citizens. Online services provide citizens direct access to government and serve to promote social change by improving the opportunity for constituency input (Fountain, 2001). E-government implementations with e-feedback collection methods allow citizen participation in government in a venue other than direct personal interaction. Putnam (2000) theorized that greater citizen participation in government strengthens the fabric of representative democracy.

Recommendations for Action and Further Study

Practitioners within the field of local government in both metropolitan and micropolitan statistical areas in the United States need to identify best practices within e-government, e-feedback, and auditing e-feedback to maximize citizen satisfaction with government. Any recommendation for further study may build on the foundation of Norris and Lloyd's (2006) call for the field of public administration to focus on theory development and testing and Coursey and Norris's (2008) encouragement of the collection of empirical data. Results of this study suggest five specific recommendations:

1. At this point, the most straightforward recommendation for further study would be to modify the survey questionnaire into an online format and begin a longitudinal survey project. Research into e-feedback needs to expand beyond the collection of descriptive information into an ongoing analysis of the factors that both contribute to interactive online government websites and support iterative feedback cycles.

2. Stratified results by population or budget could not be used to compare or evaluate differences based on the response rate. A future study could identify specific areas of study by population or budget to determine if differences exist between the implementation strategies of e-government, e-feedback, and auditing e-feedback throughout local governments.

3. A more focused case study using directed question interviews could generate a deeper level of understanding about a specific municipality.

4. Regional sampling could provide an expansion of the current study to focus on a specific area of the country.

5. A revised examination of the composite variables used to represent e-government, e-feedback, and auditing e-feedback could be used to enhance future studies.

Concluding Statement

Although at first glance these findings might not seem inherently revolutionary to some, they do clearly set a foundation for further research. Building on the theories of Lindahl (2010) and Aikins (2008) that the landscape of e-government, e-feedback, and auditing e-feedback has been established, researchers conducting further studies can begin to define best practices utilizing the baseline research collected in this study. Every category or variable tested herein demonstrated potential for future expansion based on the degree of expected future implementation.

Overall e-government appeared to be implemented at a rate of 48% with a potential future expansion to 72%. The degree of e-feedback implementation was slightly lower at 42% with an expected expansion to 61%, but within local governments specific e-feedback mechanisms are being utilized to benefit citizen participation within local government. The greatest potential for expansion exists within local government utilization of auditing from e-feedback mechanisms, given the current rate of 32% implementation with a potential expansion to less than half of all local governments. With only 44% of all local governments expecting to implement auditing using e-feedback methods, a large window for improvement exists. Overall, the results of the study clearly show that possibilities exist for local governments to maximize citizen satisfaction by utilizing e-feedback and auditing e-feedback methods to increase interactivity through both synchronous and asynchronous communication.

References

Aikins, S. K. (2008). *Research in internet-based citizen participation: The unrealized promise of bringing citizens closer to their governments.* La Vergne, TN: Lambert Academic.

Aikins, S. K., & Krane, D. (2005, September). *Is the promise of citizen-centered e-government limited? A multi-state analysis of municipal administrators' motivations and actions.* Paper presented at the Public Management Research Conference, Los Angeles, CA.

Ammons, D. N. (2002). *Tools for decision making: A practical guide for local government.* Washington, DC: CQ Press.

Asgarkhani, M. (2005). Digital government and its effectiveness in public management reform. *Public Management Review, 7*(3), 465-487.

Austin, J. E. (2000). *The collaboration challenge: How nonprofits and businesses succeed through strategic alliances.* San Francisco, CA: Jossey-Bass.

Babbie, E. R. (2002). *The basics of social research* (2nd ed.). Belmont, CA: Wadsworth Thompson Learning.

Babbie, E. R. (2004). *The practice of social research* (10th ed.). Belmont, CA: Wadsworth Thompson Learning.

Banerjee, D., Cronan, T. P., & Jones, T. W. (1998). Modeling IT ethics: A study in situational ethics, *MIS Quarterly, 22*, 31-60.

Bannister, F. (2007). The curse of the benchmark: An assessment of the validity and value of e-government comparisons. *International Review of Administrative Sciences, 73*(2), 171-188.

Barber, B. R. (1984). *Strong democracy: Participatory politics for a new age.* Berkeley: University of California Press.

Barlow, J., & Moller, C. (1996). *A complaint is a gift: Using customer feedback as a strategic tool.* San Francisco, CA: Berrett-Koehler.

Barrett, K., & Greene, R. (2001). *Powering up: How public managers can take control of information technology.* Washington, DC: CQ Press.

Barry, R. (2004). Web sites as recordkeeping and "recordmaking" systems. *Information Management Journal, 38*(6), 26-32.

Bartlett, J. E., Kotrlik, J. W., & Higgins, C. C. (2001). Organizational research: Determining appropriate sample size in survey.

Information Technology, Learning, and Performance Journal, 19(1), 43-50.

Baum, C. H., & Di Maio, A. (2000). *Gartner's four phases of e-government model*. Retrieved from http://www.gartner.com

Beck, R. (2003, March 10). E-gov managers map ways to prove projects' success. *Federal Times, 39*, p. 16.

Belanger, F., & Carter, L. (2009). The impact of the digital divide on e-government use. *Communications of the ACM, 52*(4), 132-135.

Bertilsson, K., & Nilsson, H. E. (2004). The power of using automatic device optimization, based on iterative device simulations, in design of high-performance devices, *Solid-State Electronics, 48*, 1721-1725.

Blair, B. (2003, April 21). Poll: Public likes e-gov but fears for privacy. *Federal Times, 39,* p. 4.

Blumenthal, M. M. (2005). Toward an open-source methodology: What we can learn from the Blogosphere. *Public Opinion Quarterly, 69*(5), 655-669.

Bovaird, T. (2003). E-government and e-governance: Organizational implications, options and dilemmas. *Public Policy and Administration, 18*(2), 37-56.

Bretschneider, S. (2003). Information technology, e-government, and institutional change. *Public Administration Review, 63*(6), 738-741.

Brudney, J. L., & Selden, S. C. (1995). The adoption of innovation by smaller local governments: The case of computer technology. *American Review of Public Administration, 25*(1), 71-86.

Calista, D. J., & Melitski, J. (2007). E-government and e-governance: Converging constructs of public sector information and communications technologies. *Public Administration Quarterly, 31*(1), 87-120.

Chambers, S. A. (2005). Democracy and (the) public(s): Spatializing politics in the internet age. *Political Theory, 33*(1), 125-136.

Chrislip, D. D., & Larson, C. E. (1994). *Collaborative leadership: How citizens and civic leaders can make a difference.* San Francisco, CA: Jossey-Bass.

Christensen, C. M., Anthony, S. D., & Roth, E. A. (2004). *Seeing what's next: Using the theories of innovation to predict industry change.* Boston, MA: Harvard Business School Press.

Cochran, W. G. (1977). *Sampling techniques* (3rd ed.). New York, NY: John Wiley & Sons.

Coleman, S. (2005). Blogs and the new politics of listening. *Political Quarterly, 76*(2), 272-280.

Coleman, S., & Moss, G. (2008). Governing at a distance—Politicians in the blogosphere. *Information Polity: The International Journal of Government & Democracy in the Information Age, 13*(1/2), 7-20.

Coleman, S., & Wright, S. (2008). Political blogs and representative democracy. *Information Polity: The International Journal of Government & Democracy in the Information Age, 13*(1/2), 1-5.

Cooper, D. R., & Schindler, P. S. (2003). *Business research methods* (8th ed.). New York, NY: Irwin McGraw-Hill.

Coursey, D., & Norris, D. F. (2008). Models of e-government: Are they correct? An empirical assessment. *Public Administration Review, 68*(3), 523-536.

Dalehite, E. G. (2008). Determinants of performance measurement: An investigation into the decision to conduct citizen surveys. *Public Administration Review, 68*(5), 891-907.

Davis, C. N. (2005). Reconciling privacy and access interests in e-government. *International Journal of Public Administration, 28*(7/8), 567-580.

Davis, F. D. (1989). Perceived usefulness, perceived ease of use, and user acceptance of information technology. *MIS Quarterly, 13*(3), 319-340.

Davis, R. (1999) *The web of politics: The Internet's impact on the American political system.* New York, NY: Oxford University Press.

Dionne, E. J. (1998). *Community works: The revival of civil society in America.* Washington, DC: Brookings Institution Press.

Dugan, R. E. (2002). Information technology budgets and costs: Do you know what your information technology costs each year? *Journal of Academic Librarianship, 28*(4), 238-243.

Dugdale, A., Daly, A., Papandrea, F., & Maley, M. (2005). Accessing e-government: challenges for citizens and organizations. *International Review of Administrative Sciences, 71*(1), 109-118.

Eisenstein, E. L. (1979). *The printing press as an agent of change: Communications and cultural transformations in early modern Europe.* New York, NY: Cambridge University

Press.

Elifson, K. W., Runyon, R. P., & Haber, A. (1998) *Fundamentals of social statistics* (3rd ed.). New York, NY: McGraw Hill.

Foster, G. D. (1981). Law, morality, and the public servant. *Public Administration Review, 41*(1), 29-34.

Fountain, J. E. (2001). *Building the virtual state: information technology and institutional change.* Washington, DC: Brookings Institution Press.

Frederickson, H. G. (1997). *The spirit of public administration.* San Francisco, CA: Jossey-Bass.

Freed, M. N., Ryan, J. M., & Hess, R. K. (1991). *Handbook of statistical procedures and their computer applications to education and the behavioral sciences.* New York, NY: American Council on Education and Macmillan Series on Higher Education.

Galindo, F. (2004). Electronic government from the legal point of view: Methods. *International Review of Law, Computers & Technology, 18*(1), 7-23.

Gladwell, M. (2005). *Blink: The power of thinking without thinking.* New York, NY: Little, Brown.

Glynn, C. J., Herbst, S., O'Keefe, G. J., & Shapiro, R. Y. (1999). *Public opinion.* Boulder, CO: Westview Press.

Haas, T. (2005). From "public journalism" to the "public's journalism"? Rhetoric and reality in the discourse on weblogs. *Journalism Studies, 6*(3), 387-396.

Hanson, C. M. (2003). The promise of democracy's college: Town hall meetings as a teaching method. *Community College Journal of Research & Practice, 27*(3), 173-190.

Hassett, W. L., & Watson, D. J. (2003). Citizen surveys: A component of the budgetary process. *Journal of Public Budgeting, Accounting & Financial Management, 15*(4), 525-541.

Hernon, P. (1994). *Statistics: A component of the research process* (Rev. ed.). Norwood, NJ: Ablex.

Hiller, J. S., & Belanger, F. (2001). *Privacy strategies for electronic government.* Washington, DC: IBM Center for the Business of Government. Retrieved from http://businessofgovernment/pdfs/hillerreport.pdf

Ho, A. T.-K. (2002). Reinventing local governments and the e-government initiative. *Public Administration Review, 62*(4), 434-444.

Ho, A. T.-K., & Ni, A. Y. (2004). Explaining the adoption of e-government features: A case study of Iowa county treasurers' offices. *American Review of Public Administration, 34*(2), 164-180.

Hunt, S. D., Sparkman, S. D., & Wilcox, J. B. (1982). The pretest in survey research: Issues and preliminary findings. *Journal of Marketing Research, 19*(2), 269-273.

Kaye, B. K. (2005). It's a blog, blog, blog world: Users and uses of weblogs. *Atlantic Journal of Communication, 13*(2), 73-95.

Kelly, J. M., & Swindell, D. (2002). Service quality variation across urban space: First steps toward a model of citizen satisfaction. *Journal of Urban Affairs, 24*(3), 271-288.

Kerbel, M. R., & Bloom, J. D. (2005). Blog for America and civic involvement. *Harvard International Journal of Press/Politics, 10*(4), 3-27.

Klingner, D. E. (2003). Technology transfer and the future of public administration: An agenda for study and practice. *Comparative Technology Transfer and Society, 1*(2), 121-145.

Koh, C. E., Ryan, S., & Prybutok, V. R. (2005). Creating value through managing knowledge in an e-government to constituency (G2C) environment. *Journal of Computer Information Systems, 45*(4), 32-41.

Kunstelj, M., & Vintar, M. (2004). Evaluating the progress of e-government development: A critical analysis. *Information Polity: The International Journal of Government & Democracy in the Information Age, 9*(3/4), 131-148.

Layne, K., & Lee, J. (2001). Developing fully functional e-government: A four stage model. *Government Information Quarterly, 18*(2), 122-136.

Levey, R. H. (2005). Politicians and the unlimited spamming of America. *Direct, 17*(16), 19-26.

Lindahl, N. (2010, April). *Transparent measurement of responsive e-government websites using automated survey techniques.* Paper presented at the meeting of the American Society for Public Administration, San Jose, CA.

Lindblom, C. E. (1959). The science of "muddling through." *Public Administration Review, 19*(2), 79-88.

MacDougall, R. (2005). Identity, electronic ethos, and blogs: A technologic analysis of symbolic exchange on the new news medium. *American Behavioral Scientist, 49*(4), 575-599.

Macedo, S. (2005). *Democracy at risk: How political choices undermine citizen participation and what we can do about it.* Washington, DC: Brookings Institution Press.

Mangione, T. W. (1995). *Mail surveys: Improving the quality.* Thousand Oaks, CA: Sage.

Markle Foundation. (2001). *Toward a framework for Internet accountability.* Retrieved October 20, 2005, from http://www.markle.org/downloadable_assets/accountability_foresumintro.pdf

Margolis, M., & Resnick, D. (2000). *Politics as usual: the cyberspace "revolution."* Thousand Oaks, CA: Sage.

McKenna, L. (2007). "Getting the word out": Policy bloggers use their soap box to make change. *Review of Policy Research, 24*(3), 209-229.

McLean, S. L., Schultz, D. A., & Steger, M. B. (2002). *Social capital: Critical perspectives on community and "Bowling Alone."* New York, NY: New York University Press.

McNabb, D. E. (2002). *Research methods in public administration and nonprofit management: Quantitative and qualitative approaches.* New York, NY: M. E. Sharpe.

Melkers, J., & Thomas, J. C. (1998). What do administrators think citizens think? Administrator predictions as an adjunct to citizen surveys. *Public Administration Review, 58*(4), 327-334.

Moon, M. J. (2002). The evolution of e-government among municipalities: Rhetoric or reality? *Public Administration Review, 62*(4), 424-433.

Moon, M. J., & Bretschneider, S. (2002). Does perception of red tape constrain IT innovativeness in organizations? Unexpected results from simultaneous equation model and implications. *Journal of Public Administration Research and Theory, 12*(2), 273-291.

Moon, M. J., & Norris, D. F. (2005). Does managerial orientation matter? The adoption of reinventing government and e-government at the municipal level. *Information Systems Journal, 15*(1), 43-60.

Moynihan, D. P. (2004). Building secure elections: E-voting, security, and systems theory. *Public Administration Review, 64*(5), 515-528.

Narayan, G. (2007). Addressing the digital divide: E-governance and m-governance in a hub and spoke model. *Electronic Journal on Information Systems in Developing Countries, 31*(1), 1-14.

Narayan, G., & Nerurkar, A. (2006). Value-proposition of e-governance services: Bridging rural–urban digital divide in developing countries. *Electronic Journal on Information Systems in Developing Countries, 2*(3), 33-44.

Norris, D. F., & Kraemer, K. L. (1996). Mainframe and PC computing in American myths and realities. *Public Administration Review, 56*(6), 568-576.

Norris, D. F., & Lloyd, B. A. (2006). The scholarly literature on e-government: characterizing a nascent field. *International Journal of Electronic Government Research, 2*(4), 40-56.

Norris, D. F., & Moon, M. J. (2005). Advancing e-government at the grassroots: Tortoise or hare? *Public Administration Review, 65*, 64-75.

Norusis, M. J. (2002). *SPSS 11.0 guide to data analysis.* Upper Saddle River, NJ: Prentice Hall.

Noveck, B. S. (2004). The future of citizen participation in the electronic state. *Journal of Law and Policy for the Information Society, 1*(1). 1-32.

Perritt, H. H., Jr. (1997). Cyberspace self-government: Town hall democracy or rediscovered royalism? *Berkeley Technology Law Journal, 12*(2), 413-475.

Poister, T. H., & Henry, G. T. (1994). Citizen ratings of public and private service quality: A comparative perspective. *Public Administration Review, 54*(2), 155-160.

Putnam, R. D. (2000). *Bowling alone: The collapse and revival of American community.* New York, NY: Simon & Schuster.

Ronaghan, S.A. (2001). *Benchmarking e-government: A global perspective.* New York, NY: United Nations Division for Public Economics and Public Administration and American Society for Public Administration. Retrieved from http://unpan1.un .org/intradoc/groups/public/documents/UN/UNPAN021547.pdf

Salkind, N. J. (1997). *Exploring research* (3rd ed.). Upper Saddle River, NJ: Prentice Hall.

Sennett, R. (1992). *The fall of public man.* New York, NY: Norton.

Siapera, E. (2008). The political subject of blogs. *Information Polity: The International Journal of Government & Democracy in the Information Age, 13*(1/2), 51-63.

Sirianni, C., & Friedland, L. (2001). *Civic innovation in America:*

*Community empowerment, public policy, and the movement
for civic renewal.* Berkeley: University of California Press.

Skocpol, T. (2003). *Diminished democracy: From membership to
management in American civic life.* Norman: University of
Oklahoma Press.

Streib, G. D., & Navarro, I. (2006). Citizen demand for interactive e-
government: The case of Georgia consumer services.
American Review of Public Administration, 36(3), 288-300.

Streib, G. D., & Willoughby, K. G. (2005). Local governments as e-
governments: meeting the implementation challenge. *Public
Administration Quarterly, 29*(1), 78-110.

Thomas, J. C., & Streib, G. (2003). The new face of government:
Citizen-initiated contacts in the era of e-government. *Journal
of Public Administration Research & Theory, 13*(1), 83-102.

Thomas, J. C., & Streib, G. (2005). E-democracy, e-commerce, and
e-research: Examining the electronic ties between citizens
and governments. *Administration & Society, 37*(3), 259-280.

Tolbert, C. J., & Mossberger, K. (2006). The effects of e-government
on trust and confidence in government. *Public Administration
Review, 66*(3), 354-369.

Trammell, K. D., Williams, A. P., Postelnicu, M., & Landreville, K.
D. (2006). Evolution of online campaigning: Increasing
interactivity in candidate websites and blogs through text and
technical features. *Mass Communication and Society, 9*(1),
21-44.

Trottier, T., Van Wart, M., & Wang, X. (2008). Examining the nature
and significance of leadership in government organizations.
Public Administration Review, 68(2), 319-333.

Van Ryzin, G. G. (2004). Expectations, performance, and citizen
satisfaction with urban services. *Journal of Policy Analysis &
Management, 23*(3), 433-448.

Van Til, J. (2000). *Growing civil society: From nonprofit sector to
third space.* Bloomington: Indiana University Press.

Van Wart, M. (2003). Public-sector leadership theory: An
assessment. *Public Administration Review, 63*(2), 214-228.

Varoga, C. (2005). Maximizing resources for a congressional
campaign. *Campaigns & Elections, 26*(3), 53-53.

Waugh, W. L., & Streib, G. (2006). Collaboration and leadership for
effective emergency management. *Public Administration
Review, 66,* 131-140.

Weigel, D. (2005). Blogging down the money trail. *Campaigns &*

Elections, 26(9), 19-22.

Welch, E. W., Hinnant, C. C., & Moon, M. J. (2005). Linking citizen satisfaction with e-government and trust in government. *Journal of Public Administration Research & Theory, 15*(3), 371-391.

Wescott, C. (2001). E-government in the Asia-Pacific region. *Asian Journal of Political Science, 9*(2), 1-24.

West, D. M. (2004). E-government and the transformation of service delivery and citizen attitudes. *Public Administration Review, 64*(1), 15-27.

Whitman, D. (1998). *The optimism gap: The I'm OK—They're not syndrome and the myth of American decline.* New York, NY: Walker.

Whitney, W. H. (2004). Digital politics: Plumbing the Net's power. *Columbia Journalism Review, 42*(6), 9.

Wichowsky, A., & Moynihan, D. P. (2008). Measuring how administration shapes citizenship: A policy feedback perspective on performance management. *Public Administration Review, 68*(5), 908-931.

Williams, A. P., Trammell, K. D., Postelnicu, M., Landreville, K. D., & Martin, J. D. (2005). Blogging and hyperlinking: Use of the web to enhance viability during the 2004 US campaign. *Journalism Studies, 6*(2), 177-186.

Wong, W., & Welch, E. (2004). Does e-government promote accountability? A comparative analysis of website openness and government accountability. *Governance, 17*, 275-197.

Ya Ni, A., & Bretschneider, S. (2007). The decision to contract out: A study of contracting for e-government services in state governments. *Public Administration Review, 67*(3), 531-544.

Yu-Che, C., & Thurmaier, K. (2008). Advancing e-government: Financing challenges and opportunities. *Public Administration Review, 68*(3), 537-548.

About the Author

Nels Lindahl is the founder of and maintains www.civichonors.com, which advocates development of ways to strengthen the community through volunteering networks. Nels received a master's degree in public administration from the University of Kansas and is currently holds a Ph.D. in public policy and administration from Walden University.

www.ingramcontent.com/pod-product-compliance
Lightning Source LLC
Chambersburg PA
CBHW081832280526
45789CB00007B/2427